DEAR KATIE

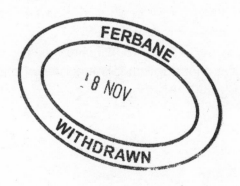

Orion

ABOUT THE AUTHOR

Katie Thistleton lives with her boyfriend Alex in Manchester, England, where she grew up. Katie is a trained journalist and has always wanted to be a writer – some of her earliest work dates back to when she was six years old!

Katie studied English and Creative Writing at Salford University. She has been a TV and radio presenter since 2013 and is best known for her work on CBBC and BBC Radio 1. Katie believes in talking (even if she did get told off for talking too much in school) and has always wanted to help people feel better. This book is inspired by the people she cares about: her nieces and nephews, her young fans and her family, who gave her much advice and support while growing up. In particular, her mum and dad, Mr and Mrs Thistleton, and her siblings – sister Sharon, brother Stephen and brother-in-law Nigel.

Find Katie on Instagram @katiethistleton and on Twitter @KatieThistleton.

DEAR KATIE

KATIE THISTLETON

With Dr Radha Modgil and Sally Angel

Orion

For my best friends Danielle, Anthony, Harry, Jennifer and Jack – who fill my life with so much happiness, and will always have my support.

For everyone who wrote to me.

Sally Angel would like to acknowledge Paul Margrie
for his support and unnerving ability to make
connections on lots of different levels

ORION CHILDREN'S BOOKS

First published in Great Britain in 2018 by Orion Children's Books

1 3 5 7 9 10 8 6 4 2

Text copyright © Katie Thistleton, 2018

A CIP catalogue record for this book
is available from the British Library.

ISBN 978 1 5101 0213 2

Printed and bound in Great Britain by Clays Ltd, St Ives plc

The paper and board used in this book are made
from wood from responsible sources.

Orion Children's Books
An imprint of
Hachette Children's Group
Part of Hodder and Stoughton
Carmelite House
50 Victoria Embankment
London EC4Y 0DZ

An Hachette UK Company
www.hachette.co.uk

www.hachettechildrens.co.uk

INTRODUCTION

Hello! Katie here, and for those of you who don't know me, I'm a TV and radio presenter who has been working with young people for many years now. I'm twenty-eight years old, but a teenage girl at heart, and throughout my childhood and teenage years I struggled at times with my emotions and mental health. I have experienced very low self-esteem, anxiety and depression. Over the past couple of years, I have learned that feeling tons of different emotions on a daily basis is totally human. In fact, it can't be avoided. It's important to embrace the different thoughts, feelings and emotions we experience, and remember that we can't always be happy! Sadness, anger and fear all serve a purpose and make us who we are, and feeling those sorts of emotions allows us to truly enjoy happiness when it comes.

Often we don't talk about it when life throws up feelings which we find hard to deal with, because we are ashamed or embarrassed we feel that way. We assume we are on our own in those feelings, but we're definitely not. When writing this book I realised that most of us go through our own very unique versions of the same emotional struggles. I've discovered methods, tips and tricks that help me feel good about myself most of the time, and I want to help you do the same.

I used to love reading 'agony aunt' pages in magazines when I was younger – there's something wonderfully comforting about discovering that someone else understands or feels the same way that you do. They often give practical advice which can help us, because while every problem is specific to each person, we experience lots of the same things. You should never feel alone – there's always help available.

In order to write this book, I asked 10–16 year olds to write to me anonymously about any problems they were having. I visited schools to meet with young people and invited them to email me to ask for advice. I received tons of emails and I cannot thank those of you who have contributed enough. I have had an amazing, honest insight into what young people are going through in today's world, and much of it took me way back to my childhood and teen years. Some of it is still relevant to the way I feel now.

I spotted lots of common themes when reading your letters, and I have tried to include all the different types of problems I came across. I hope that reading this book will help you learn to love yourself and be resilient enough to deal with whatever life throws at you. I also hope it shows you that whatever you're going through, you're not the only one. My idea is that this will be a book you can return to time and time again as you experience different things throughout the stages of your life. I've included exercises and places for you to take notes so you can make this book your own.

I haven't written this book alone – I've had help from some brilliant experts, and you can find out about them in the next section. If you need more immediate help, there are handy helplines at the back of the book. You can access more advice on the *Dear Katie* YouTube channel.

Enjoy reading, fellow humans!

Love,
Katie xxx

P.S. This book only contains broad general advice and should not be seen as a substitute for medical advice. If you have any concerns about your physical or mental health, please seek advice/help from a GP or mental health professional.

P.P.S. The letters in this book are based on those from real children and teenagers, however they have been edited to ensure the anonymity of writers, and also for sense, clarity, length or to focus on one particular issue.

THE 'DEAR KATIE' EXPERTS

OUR DOCTOR: DR RADHA MODGIL

Dr Radha is a practising NHS GP in London and a campaigner for physical and mental wellbeing. She is best known for her work broadcasting on BBC Radio 1, Channel 4, BBC Three and CBBC. Currently writing for the i newspaper, Top of the Pops magazine and BBC Advice, she has also contributed to online projects including BBC iWonder and BBC Learning.Radha has worked on health promotion campaigns with Public Health England, MIND, The Mix and the NHS Youth Forum. She has a real passion to help young people empower themselves with the skills they need to stay physically and emotionally healthy.

Find Dr Radha @DrRadhaModgil on Twitter and @dr_radha on Instagram.

OUR PSYCHOTHERAPIST: SALLY ANGEL

Sally Angel is a BACP accredited psychotherapist and combines working as a psychotherapist with being a TV producer. She studied languages at Cambridge University and Psychotherapy at the Centre for Counselling and Psychotherapy Education in London.

She's passionate about psychotherapy and believes that with a better understanding of our mind, body and emotions, we can help ourselves and each other. She regularly meditates, practices yoga and tai chi, writes and loves walking in nature.

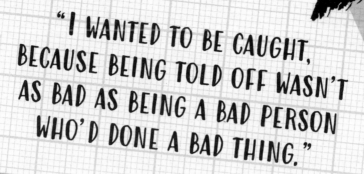

"I WANTED TO BE CAUGHT, BECAUSE BEING TOLD OFF WASN'T AS BAD AS BEING A BAD PERSON WHO'D DONE A BAD THING."

Dear Katie,

Help me to choose to do the right thing.

From Me

Hey You,

Thanks for your letter. It stood out among all the letters I received. It's brilliantly simple and uncomplicated, yet not-so-simple and very complicated – all at the same time.

The first time I remember learning about doing the right thing was when I was about five years old. I was going shopping with my mum, and on the way we nipped into the chemist. I can't remember what for, but that's not relevant – my family's ailments didn't concern me at the ripe old age of five. What did concern me, was getting a freebie out of every situation. It's the reason Happy Meals and Kinder Eggs are so successful. Getting a new toy is the epitome of success when you're a child.

Pharmacies are boring places. They don't tend to sell toys. Sometimes they don't even sell sweets or chocolate – the closest you might get to something fun in a chemist are some cough sweets or cartoon plasters. On this particular day I had brought a little wicker handbag out on our shopping trip. The bag actually belonged to one of my dolls but I really wanted to play at being a grown-up that day, so I donned my little doll's bag and trotted down to the shops with my mum. I felt sophisticated, so what would I do next? I decided a great addition to my new, grown-up lifestyle would be one of the hairbrushes sitting in a discount basket by the door. Grown-up ladies had hairbrushes in their handbags sometimes. I knew this. I'd seen them. I wanted one too. So I put one of the hairbrushes in my bag, and walked out of the shop without Mum noticing.

About ten minutes later, as we strolled down the street, my mum turned to find me brushing my hair with my new brush, label still intact, as I walked along. Needless to say, Mum was not best pleased about her thieving daughter taking the hairbrush without paying. But we were almost at the shops, and quite far away from the chemist by now. It was the perfect crime – no one would guess that sweet, five-year-old Katie had been on a stealing spree that day – and we could have probably gotten away with it. But no – Mum marched me all the way back to the chemist on my little legs. She confessed to the pharmacy staff that I had stolen the hairbrush, and made me apologise and give it back.

That was the first time I remember learning a lesson about right and wrong, but actually, now I think about it, I already knew. My instincts told me what I'd done was wrong and I think that's why I started using the brush so boldly, because I almost wanted to be caught. I wanted to confess and I wanted redemption. If I had kept the stealing a secret for longer, if I'd taken the brush home and secretly used it in my bedroom, I would have owned up to the theft before too long. I wouldn't have wanted to harbour the feeling that I had wronged somebody else, and wronged myself by being someone I didn't really want to be. I didn't want to be a thief. I wanted to be caught, because being told off wasn't as bad as being a bad person who'd done a bad thing. Someone who'd lied and got away with it. Short-term difficulty equals a long-term clean conscience – do whatever means you can live with yourself the most.

I could sit and give you example after example of times people have done the right thing. I could tell you about people doing the wrong thing, and then realising it was wrong and making amends, like five-year-old Katie and the hairbrush. I could also give you some practical ways that you can use to come up with a conclusion, such as making a list of pros and cons, imagining different possible outcomes, 'sleeping on it' before coming to a decision, asking others what they would do, or simply considering the greater good. These might help you, but chances are, the thing you thought was the right thing to do before you read my reply to your letter would probably be the same thing as what you now think afterwards. Just like I knew stealing a hairbrush was wrong before I did it, then felt bad and got not-so-accidentally caught red-handed.

There's a philosopher called Jeremy Bentham who founded something called 'utilitarianism'. He said, "The greatest happiness of the greatest number is the foundation of morals and legislation." In other words, he believed that in any situation you should choose whatever will benefit the wellbeing of most people. I learned about this theory when I was studying philosophy at college. Our teacher presented us with a dilemma: if someone held a gun to your head and said, "You must kill your dad, otherwise we will kill a whole building full of innocent people," what would you do? Bentham would argue that you should kill your own father. It's a good theory, albeit a ridiculous and unlikely imaginary situation, but it caused great debate amongst the class. A few of us agreed that yes, it made much more sense to kill one father in order to save a whole building full of innocent people who could go on to live fulfilling lives. But in reality, I wouldn't kill my father. I'm a human being, and I'm selfish, and I love my dad. In any situation I will always do whatever is right for myself and the people I love. I will always do what I deem to be the right thing.

You should do that too.

Love,
Katie xxx

NOTES

> ## "FAMILIES ARE COMPLICATED BECAUSE THEY'RE MADE UP OF HUMANS, AND HUMANS ARE COMPLICATED."

Dear Katie,

I'm worried my mum doesn't like me very much and wonder if it would have been better for everyone if I hadn't been born. My mum and dad split up a couple of years ago and now my mum has had a baby with her new boyfriend. I like her boyfriend and he's nice to me, but both of them love my baby brother more than they love me. I think they would be happier if I wasn't around – then they could be a perfect family. My mum tells me she loves me, but what if she doesn't?

From Me

Hey You,

Have you ever seen the film *It's a Wonderful Life*? It's one of my favourite films, and set at Christmas, so it's often shown on TV during the festive season. It's in black and white, but don't let that put you off. It's about a man who thinks the world would be a better place if he hadn't been born. He's a grown-up, so his problems are very different to yours. He has made some mistakes which mean he is struggling financially, and he believes his family would be much happier and better off if he wasn't around.

In the film, an angel shows him what life would have been like had he not been born. You can probably guess the reason for this – the angel shows him how life would have actually been considerably worse for his loved ones. He's a good person and didn't realise that all the little things he's done in his life – sometimes very small actions – have made a big impact on others. All lives are like that. Your life is like that. The smile you give to someone in a supermarket, saying hi to a friend, looking after a sibling – all those little actions mean more than you know and might have a knock-on effect that changes lives for the better.

Before we get into the nitty-gritty of your family situation, something I really want you to know is how important you are as a person on your own. You want friends and family members who love you and who you love, but I don't want you to forget that there are many places in life we can find love and happiness. Even if your mum didn't love you, or if she did love your brother more than you, you would still be able to continue with your life and do all the things you want to do. You could still focus on the things that matter to you, make yourself feel good and love yourself. Your mother has raised you but you are a person who can live, do what you want to do and find happiness all on your own.

Now we've established that, I'll move on to your family. Really, from the little I know about your situation, it sounds as though they definitely do love you. Your mum tells you she loves you. Your stepdad is nice to you. There is no 'perfect' family. Some people's parents are still together, some people's aren't, some people have lost family members or have adopted family members or are adopted themselves. Some people have ten siblings and some have no siblings and some only have one parent. Some have two mums and some have two dads – I even know a family where the child has FOUR mums and two dads. Families are complicated because they're made up of humans, and humans are complicated. Your mother and stepdad won't be thinking that their family would be perfect if it wasn't for you, because life isn't about writing down a perfect plan and sticking to it. There's no point in deciding: "I'm going to marry one person, have two children and a dog with them and stay with them for ever." Things can change – sometimes people split up and meet other people and have children with their new partners – but we will always want people who bring love and happiness into our lives. Your mum won't love you any less now that she isn't with your dad and has a new baby with your stepdad. She's just going to love the baby as well. But she still loves you.

I want to say, it's totally understandable that you're having these insecure feelings of doubt. It's a difficult thing to go through your parents splitting up, and I'm sorry you've had to experience that. It can help to talk to your family about how you feel, because divorces and break-ups are hard on everyone and often you can help each other to get through it.

Also, remember that you are the big sister. That doesn't make you inferior, but actually makes you very special. I'm the baby of my family, and when I was younger I sometimes resented my older sister, because I assumed that since she was the first to exist, she was the most special one. Whether you're the oldest or the youngest or somewhere in between, it's likely you will experience feelings of jealousy and insecurity at times. Lots of us worry that we might not be loved enough or might not fit in when we're growing up. I remember worrying that I was adopted because I was the only one in my family with blonde hair! Looking back, it wouldn't even have mattered if I had been adopted, because my family still loved me very much.

Your baby brother will be getting lots of attention at the moment because he can't do anything on his own. Babies are helpless, and humans are hard-wired to find babies cute because it ensures we look after the young and vulnerable, who need us to care for them. They can't survive without us. It's the same reason we like kittens and puppies. But this will change eventually. Your brother will grow up and be able to do things for himself one day. And, in the meantime, it doesn't make you any less important. Celebrate yourself and all the things you can do that he can't. Sure, he might be able to make people coo and smile and speak in a high-pitched voice, but you can have a conversation with your parents, you can help them out and you can do things for yourself to bring yourself happiness.

Sometimes, when we are jealous, we isolate ourselves from the situation and this makes us feel even more insecure. But this baby is YOUR brother – you're one of his closest family members! Rather than feeling pushed out, you have a role to play here. You get to help bring this baby up! You get to teach him, and play with him, and he's going to look up to you and adore you as his older sibling.

Seeing as you can have a conversation with your mum (because you're not a stupid baby, lol), why don't you chat to her about how you're feeling? She is probably super-overwhelmed with all the new responsibility and lack of sleep which comes with having a newborn, and might not have realised you're feeling this way. I'm sure that she loves you, and having a chat together about this might make you both feel really good.

Love,
Katie xxx

THERAPIST SALLY SAYS

We often fantasise about the perfect family – but it doesn't really exist. Life is messy and changing all the time. New babies are time-consuming, not love-consuming, just as we all were when we were little. It's hard not to feel a bit pushed out when new babies come along and when so many changes are going on, but the thing about love is that it's pretty infinite and the more we give the more we have.

As families change and grow it's important to take time and space to find your place in your new family. Communicating is key, so keep talking to friends, family and maybe even your teachers. Don't bottle up your feelings, because they'll only come out in another form. If you can't find anyone to talk to yet, try writing down what you feel – and then read what you've written, with love and compassion, as if you are your own best friend. Then just tear them up after you've written them.

NOTES

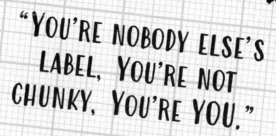

"YOU'RE NOBODY ELSE'S LABEL, YOU'RE NOT CHUNKY, YOU'RE YOU."

Dear Katie,

My stepdad always makes jokes about me and they are starting to upset me. He calls me 'chunky' because I am a bit of a chubby girl, and even though he's joking I'm feeling a bit sick of it. He's always nice to me and looks after me, and I know it's just his sense of humour because he is the same with my stepbrother. My stepdad always tells him he will never get a girlfriend and my brother makes jokes to him back, but I don't feel like I can do that. It's making me not want to eat in front of him, in case he calls me fatty or something, especially if I have crisps or chocolate. What can I do to stop it from bothering me?

From Me

Hey You,

Comedy, eh? There are lots of comedians whose style is to make jokes at other people's expense – and it sounds like your stepdad fancies himself as one of these!

I have had friends who've made me feel rubbish about myself. I used to have a friend who worked in fashion when I was at university. She would always comment on the clothes I wore, on my make-up, and sometimes on my weight and eating habits. At the time I would appear to take on her advice, smile and nod and put up with it, but when I got home I always felt really deflated and rubbish about myself. I started to realise that I didn't look forward to spending time with her. But I didn't stop, and we humans often do that – spend time with people whose company we don't actually enjoy – because we think we need to be polite. Or we worry cutting them out will be such an awkward experience that it will make us feel even worse than the feeling we have when we are with them. Or we feel like we need them. Eventually I did manage to cut this friend out of my life. Nowadays I only choose to spend time with people who make me feel good about myself, and it makes for a much happier, carefree Katie.

That said, I DO still have to spend some time with people who don't necessarily bring out the best in me. We can't always control who we spend time with – we can't control who our work colleagues are, who is in our class at school, who our teachers are, who is on our netball team or who is in our family. I feel for you, because your stepdad is in your home and home is somewhere you should feel comfortable to be yourself. You should be able to eat crisps and chocolate without feeling like you're being watched and judged. You should feel able to wear your most unflattering yet comfy nighty and not worry about someone calling you chunky.

We often let people get away with things that aren't necessarily right because it's just 'who they are'. Like a grandma who is a bit racist because it's just 'how things were in her day'. Or an idiot uncle who makes sexist jokes because 'it's just how he is'. I understand that your stepdad is a bit of a joker – I know his type, I know that he is just trying to be funny and actually, in a weird way, it might even be his way of bonding with you. But that doesn't make it right, if it's making you feel upset, annoyed or conscious of your body or your eating habits, in the comfort of your own home. For this reason you should speak to him. Find a time when he's on his own, and let him know his references to your weight are making you unhappy, even if they are only meant as jokes. If this doesn't work, or if you'd feel uncomfortable speaking to him directly about it, ask your mum, your brother or another family member to mention something instead. It might not have even crossed your stepdad's mind that the 'funny' remarks he is making are actually hurting the people in his family, and he needs to be aware of it.

It isn't fair that he also does this to your brother. Perhaps you and your bro can team up and spend a bit more time together. You might feel you can confide in each other – you're both in the same boat and it can be very therapeutic to vent to someone who has the same issue as you. It may not bother your brother, but people are different and just because someone isn't offended by something, doesn't mean you can't be. If someone's actions are having a negative effect on you then you don't need to put up with it. End of story.

You could also try spending more time with your stepdad, if this is something you'd be comfortable doing. Maybe join him when he's watching his favourite TV show, or ask him a question about something he knows about. Perhaps ask him about the book he is reading, what his job is like, or maybe for advice about something. You could try asking a question that will get him chatting, like 'Did you enjoy school when you were there?' or 'What's the favourite job you've ever had?' or 'How did you and mum meet?' I'm not sure how well you and your stepdad know each other or how close you are, but perhaps he makes these jokes because he knows of no other way to communicate with a young girl who's at a very different stage of her life. Getting to know each other better might mean you have things to talk about, and less time can be spent on jokes at your expense. Like I said, weirdly this might be his way of making an effort and showing affection to you, but it is having the very opposite effect and could actually be perceived as bullying.

When people repeatedly call us a name or put a label on us, we can be indoctrinated by it – we can start to believe it. I don't want you to believe that you should have a label based on your size. I don't want your step-brother to believe that he will never get a girlfriend, and consequently struggle to form relationships because he lacks confidence. Words are powerful and the names we call ourselves and others can really stick. I'm of the belief that you can 'talk things true'. Once, on a production of a kids' TV show with Jedward, I decided I really wanted a Nandos for lunch. A few people on the production team said there wasn't time for Nandos. I didn't want to give up on my chicken dreams, so I told Jedward and a couple of other people that I'd heard we were getting Nandos for lunch. Word spread. Everyone just took it for the truth. Guess where we ended up at lunch? Yep, you guessed it, Burger K— No, of course not – we marched on to

Nandos as if that had always been the plan and no one had disputed it.

I must add a disclaimer here to let you know that I don't condone lying. I wouldn't deceive anyone to get my own way with anything more serious than chicken wings or a caramel cheesecake. But this story demonstrates one of the experiences I've had that taught me: if you say something enough, people can make it become true. It's what we call a self-fulfilling prophecy. So don't let anyone tell you what your 'self' is – you are a complex person and whoever you want to be.

You can't control what your stepdad does, and he might not stop even with the intervention I've suggested, but you can control your reaction to him. Try not to let his negative comments get to you, while remembering that one day you won't need to be around him if you don't want to be.

I read something recently about people who make jokes either at their own expense or at the expense of others. Many stand-up comedians often make jokes about their own gender, race, accent, birthplace, body type, and so on. Psychologists say that people who make these sorts of jokes have subconsciously adopted that style of humour because of their own insecurities and issues. I'm sure most comedians would be the first to admit that this is why they make these jokes – because seeing the humour in situations they find difficult or things that bother them makes them feel a lot better about it. They find enjoyment in dealing with the trials and tribulations of life in this way.

Remember, whenever your stepdad calls you chunky, or in fact whenever ANYONE calls you ANYTHING, that it isn't anything to do with you. People only look for 'flaws' in others and point them out because they are insecure about their own bodies, lives, personalities, etc. We all worry about whether we are good enough, whether we are living our lives right, and we all deal with that in different ways. Some people try to convince themselves that others aren't as good as them, and often make other people feel bad in the process. If we all realised that we are each good enough in our own individual ways, we wouldn't need to do this. For this reason, I really respect you for saying that you can't joke back at your stepdad in the same way your brother does. Two wrongs don't make a right and picking on your stepdad in return definitely won't solve anything. Stay true to your beautiful nature and do whatever makes you happy – whether that's eating crisps and chocolate or doing cartwheels in the park – and don't let anyone make you feel bad about it. You are YOU – do what makes you feel good. Be content in the knowledge that you ARE good enough and you're ANYTHING you want to be – you're nobody else's label, you're not chunky, you're YOU.

Love,
Katie xxx

> "WHAT'S THE WORST THAT CAN HAPPEN? DESPITE HOW IT SOMETIMES FEELS, YOUR FACE WON'T OVERHEAT AND EXPLODE!"

Dear Katie,

How can I stop myself going red in class when a teacher asks me a question?

From Me

Hey You,

'Going red' is SO annoying, isn't it? What you are referring to is blushing, and it's what happens when we are embarrassed. Our cheeks, and sometimes even our whole face and neck and chest, flush a redder colour, as if you're really warm. This can occur when something embarrassing happens, or when you're upset or nervous or angry or stressed. In fact, when I was a teenager it sometimes just happened for absolutely no reason at all.

Blushing absolutely plagued my life when I was younger – I was someone who really suffered with it. Some people don't seem to blush at all, do they? But I would 'go red' whenever a teacher asked me a question in class, like you, and whenever someone spoke to me unexpectedly. Sometimes I'd blush when I had to talk to a stranger – like being served in a shop – and sometimes just when I was talking to my own parents!

The worst thing about blushing is that it happens because we are uncomfortable and embarrassed, but then the blushing itself starts to make us feel more uncomfortable and embarrassed. Sometimes other people point it out (how lovely of them), you hear whispers of 'Look how red they've gone!' and then you feel even worse about it. Before long, it becomes something you really worry about and dread, and it's even more likely to happen because it's now such a big deal to you.

I remember trying out all sorts of remedies I'd either read somewhere or just completely made up myself. I'd hold cold wet cloths to my cheeks at night, I'd wear absolutely TONS of makeup in a bid to hide my flushing cheeks. But the layers of foundation didn't work – the blushing still shone through. Then I tried putting on loads of blusher, so it looked like I was blushing ALL THE TIME and would therefore hopefully hide it when I did – but that also didn't work.

I had a friend in college who used to wear cute little trendy scarves all the time because her neck would flush when she was embarrassed or stressed. Thin scarves were really in fashion at the time so nobody guessed they were hiding something! I used to wish there was a scarf I could use to cover my cheeks. But the reality is that nothing worked for me until I tackled my blushing from within.

As the thing that makes you blush is public speaking, you could take some steps to improve your confidence in that area. The more you put yourself in situations which embarrass you, the less they affect you in the long run – you get used to them, and they're not such a big deal. So I suggest absolutely going for it – put your hand up and answer questions, talk to people in your class you don't usually speak to, perhaps even join a drama group or another after-school club that takes your fancy. I did this when I was struggling with my confidence and it really helped the blushing.

When you're putting your hand up to answer or ask a question in class, or standing up to perform in front of your drama group – just completely own that blushing. Be confident, regardless of the fact your cheeks are flushing a crimson colour. Speak clearly and confidently and don't shy away. Say to yourself: "I'm blushing, but so what? It's a bodily function and everyone does it." Be kind to yourself, and remember it's understandable that you get nervous or embarrassed sometimes and it's part of your human make-up – it's not your fault. Your classmates will be totally impressed by your confidence if they see you powering through despite the fact you're a blusher. In fact, they will probably like you more for it, since showing nerves demonstrates that we are human – it's endearing and comforting and helps you to understand someone. I always like people more after I've seen them blush, because it makes me want to be on their side. I want to say, "Oh hey there, friend, you're just like me! Let's get together and help each other through the tricky times." When I accepted that I blush and I started to sign up to situations where I would have speak in public – like answering questions in class – eventually the blushing started to go away.

If I asked you right now NOT to think about pink elephants, you would probably find it hard to not think about them, whereas if I said you were allowed to think about pink elephants then you might do so for a little while but then would soon drift on to thinking about something else. Blushing is like that too. When we make a big deal about not being allowed to do something, whether it's blushing or thinking about pink elephants, it often becomes more of a problem than if we allowed it to happen in the first place. If you're able to accept your blushing, it will likely go away more quickly than if you fight it.

As with so many annoying things you have to go through in your school years, blushing seems to be worse when you're a teenager. But it will get easier with time if you accept it, own it, do what you want to do and answer those questions regardless. (What's the worst that can happen? Despite how it sometimes feels, your face won't overheat and explode!) If grown-up Katie told teenage Katie what she does for a living these days, teenage Katie would not believe her – standing up in front of people on stages, in schools, in front of a camera presenting live telly. Teenage Katie was shy, embarrassed and blushed like a tomato, but none of that lasted for ever. Blushing stopped plaguing my life once I realised that no amount of make-up was going to cover it up, that I had to tackle it from within, and that, more importantly, I didn't need to cover it up, because it wasn't as big a deal as I told myself it was.

Remember, blusher is a type of makeup which people buy to make themselves more attractive, so it follows that blushing is actually attractive, no?

Love,
Katie xxx

DR RADHA SAYS

We don't know exactly why we blush, but there are a number of theories. One is that it helps other people to see that we are embarrassed or distressed, so they can change their behaviour towards us. Another is that blushing evolved so we would adapt our behaviour if we had done something that we should not have done. We still don't know for sure which of these is right – or if it's something else entirely!

The scientific explanation for blushing has to do with the hormone adrenaline. When you feel embarrassed or stressed, your sympathetic nervous system gets triggered and this sets off a chain of events in your body called the 'fight or flight' response. Even when the situation – like public speaking or a party – is quite harmless, if your brain interprets it as threatening, then adrenaline is released into your body, causing the blood vessels in your face to widen. This means that more blood reaches your skin, making it redder and hot – in other words, you blush. You typically blush over your face but you can also blush over your chest, neck and ears.

Factoid: Did you know that erythrophobia is the term used when people develop an excessive fear of blushing? This is sometimes linked to other anxiety disorders or social anxiety. It causes a cycle of intense fear of blushing which then leads to blushing itself.

NOTES

> **"WE CAN'T CONTROL OTHER PEOPLE AND WE CAN'T CHANGE THEIR MINDS, BUT WE CAN BE TOTALLY IN CONTROL OF HOW WE CHOOSE TO LIVE."**

Dear Katie,

I think my dad might be racist because he's said things before about people from other countries when he's watching TV, and my mum shouts at him if he says stuff like that in front of me. We have been learning about racism at school and I'm worried my dad might not be a nice person, even though in every other way he is always really nice.

From Me

Hey You,

When we are young we often think that parents are all-powerful, all-knowledgeable, invincible beings who do everything right. It's important that we do think this, because otherwise when we run out into the road as toddlers and our parents shout at us and tell us off, we might not pay any attention to them and we might not make it to five years old.

But parents are not perfect. Parents are individual people themselves – human beings just trying to get it right – and they make mistakes. When we are young we sometimes fail to realise that our parents are people too, who had whole lives of their own before we even existed, and they still have their own problems, worries, insecurities, fears, beliefs and ideas about the world. They still get things wrong.

We are all capable of hate, anger and jealousy just as much as we are capable of love, compassion and kindness. There are reasons why people are the way they are. Your dad's racism might come from issues he has with himself. People sometimes struggle to accept others because deep down they can't accept themselves. Often the people we love and respect can surprise us with some pretty ugly personality traits which we weren't expecting.

I'm sorry that you've gone through this, because it's sad when we realise that someone we look up to might not be so perfect after all.

When I was a young teenager, I was obsessed with a particular pop star and had his posters all over my room. I followed everything he did – I bought every magazine he featured in, watched every television interview, bought every CD he released and was lucky enough to go to a few of his concerts. To me he was perfect, flawless, my idol.

Then one day he was involved in a huge scandal that was all over the newspapers. He'd done something I could have never imagined him doing. I was heartbroken, not only because it meant I didn't want to marry him any more, but also because I realised I actually didn't know him that well at all. I'd made up this ideal person in my mind – the perfect friend, boyfriend, husband, father, everything. But really I had very little information about him, only the selected amount he had chosen to reveal to the world and his fans through song lyrics and interviews. The rest I'd made up – I'd latched on to this individual because something about them appealed to me and I wanted to believe the person in my head was real. But then the newspapers told me a different story. They told me this pop star was human, like everyone else, and had a made a mistake. He'd done something his fans wouldn't like, something which didn't sit with the 'perfect' image he'd been portraying. As I tore each poster down from my wall, leaving remnants of Blu-Tack behind, I realised not only that my pop-star crush wasn't perfect, but neither was anybody else.

Realising your dad isn't perfect doesn't mean you have to stop loving or respecting him. But you also don't have to agree with him. You are your own person and you have a right to form your own opinions and stand up for what you believe in. Educate yourself – watch the news, read books, read newspapers, talk to lots of different people and listen to different opinions – then form your own beliefs. It sounds like you already have, through your education about racism at school. You know what racism is and you've started to think about it and question your dad's opinions. I think that's brilliant. Not everybody would have written to me to question whether their father was right. Not everyone would have realised that Dad could be wrong. Lots of people would have simply adopted their parent's views, and that's why discrimination continues to exist.

People learn from those around them, which means your dad might learn from you. I've got friends who have worked hard to educate their parents and grandparents out of racist, sexist and homophobic beliefs. You don't need to get into an argument with your dad, but you could have a calm, grown-up, intellectual conversation with him about what you've been learning at school, and tell him what you believe. Who knows, he might just change his mind. He might have picked up his existing views from his parents or friends, and he might be able to adopt yours. Keep in mind that your dad has probably lived with these views for a long time, so you may not succeed in changing them overnight, but it's still worth sharing your opinions and challenging his perception of the world. Eventually it might make a difference.

It's often said, "Be the change you want to see in the world." We might not be able to stop wars, violence, racism and other terrible atrocities single-handedly, but we can do more than we think by living life with good ideals and sharing our views.

We can't control other people and we can't change their minds, but we can be totally in control of how we choose to live.

Love,
Katie xxx

THERAPIST SALLY SAYS

Prejudice and racism are usually based on fear and ignorance of other people. They are often are about projecting things we don't like in ourselves on to someone else. People who are racist often feel threatened by people who are different from them. They might feel unsafe and want to feel in control and is if they are "right". It's as if they would rather stay fixed in their ignorance than open their minds to new or other ways of thinking or seeing the world. You are not your dad and you have a great opportunity here to lead him by your own example and introduce him to some new ideas.

Disagreement is healthy in the right context – if you can challenge someone's beliefs without making them feel bad about who they are as a person, it can be very helpful.

> ## "WE DON'T HAVE TO DO ANYTHING WE DON'T WANT TO DO OR ANYTHING THAT DOESN'T MAKE US FEEL GOOD."

Dear Katie,

My friend showed me a video online and I can't stop thinking about it. It's made me feel really uncomfortable. He didn't seem bothered by it and I'm scared if I go to his house again he will show me more videos like that. I don't want to tell my parents I've seen it because they will be angry and I'm embarrassed to tell them what I saw.

From Me

Hey You,

I'm so sorry to hear that you've watched something which has made you feel uncomfortable. It's understandable that you can't stop thinking about it.

I can remember times I've seen disturbing things on TV or online, especially the ones I watched when I was younger. They can stick in your mind no matter what you do to forget them. Sometimes when we most want to forget something it can keep popping into our heads, keeping us awake at night or making us feel anxious. When I was younger I remember seeing distressing images on the news. They would pop into my head late at night, making me feel sick to my stomach – even writing this now I can remember some of the distressing things I saw when I was younger and they still make me feel uneasy.

Next time your friend asks if they can show you a video, say no, and explain that you didn't like watching the other video you saw. There's no shame in not wanting to watch these sorts of things, so be confident about it. If your friend teases you, stick to your guns. They might be watching the videos to appear cool and if you dismiss them they might realise it's not impressive after all, and stop doing it themselves. These sorts of things affect people in different ways – perhaps your friend has seen this kind of stuff lots before and it doesn't bother them any more. But you haven't, and you do not have to. Once you've said no, suggest that you watch or do something else instead, or change the subject. If it continues, do what you said and don't go round there – not because you're afraid, but because you don't want to spend time with someone like this. Friends who make you do things you don't want to do are not the kind of friends you want in your life. You will find other friends who will bring the best out of you, and who won't pressure you into things they want to do.

We don't have to do anything we don't want to do or anything that doesn't make us feel good. Proper friends don't make you do that and will understand when you say no. Once you've said no to peer pressure the first time, it makes it easier to do so again in the future, and your friends will know they can't walk all over you.

You have the power to make your own decisions. You are in control of what you do. Don't watch if you don't want to.

In the meantime, try to speak to someone about what you saw on this video. This can be anyone you feel comfortable talking to, so if not your parents, then a teacher, school counsellor, friend's parent, or other relative. Find a trusted adult, and tell them what you saw and how it made you feel. Remember, a lot of videos available online are not real, so an adult might be able to find out whether what you saw was pretend or not. In any case, talking about it will help you feel better and get this image out of your head. You don't ever need to deal with troubling emotions on your own – there's always someone to help.

Love,
Katie xxx

THERAPIST SALLY SAYS

Friends can sometimes show us things and without meaning to, they've taken away our freedom to choose what we look at. It can even happen when we click on a link ourselves and end up looking at something we wish we hadn't seen.

Being exposed to mature or traumatic content is nothing to be ashamed of. It's not a sign of weakness nor a reflection of inner failing. It is sometimes just something that happened without full consent.

Sometimes it's not the event itself that is harmful, but how we choose to respond to it. Maybe we feel guilty because we want to see more of it. Whatever your response is,

don't let it be a secret. If we can allow others
to help us and also be kind to ourselves along the way,
it's much better.

It's harder now to filter out inappropriate content than it
used to be. Sometimes if we see extreme content online
or in the real world we can suffer flashbacks, disturbed
sleep and generally feel a bit rubbish – if you notice any
of these signs it might be worth talking to your GP.

NOTES

_____

_____

_____

_____

_____

_____

_____

_____

_____

_____

_____

_____

_____

_____

_____

_____

> "WHEN WE COMPARE OURSELVES TO OTHERS ONLINE, WE ARE COMPARING OUR 'BEHIND THE SCENES' TO EVERYONE ELSE'S 'HIGHLIGHT REEL'."

Dear Katie,

I always compare myself to other girls, and it's driving me crazy. I can't stop thinking about whether someone has better hair than me or a better body than me and I'm always trying to find a reason why I might be better than them, but I just don't feel good enough. I compare myself to my friends on Instagram, but also to other girls I don't even know. I've just started going out with my first boyfriend and I feel really jealous whenever I see him hanging out with other girls at school, because I worry he will think they are better than me too. I feel so pathetic, but it's really getting me down.

From Me

Hey You,

There are two things I want to tell you, first and foremost:

- YOU ARE LIKE SO MANY OTHER GIRLS IN THE WORLD
- YOU ARE LIKE NO OTHER GIRL IN THE WORLD

I don't usually like to contradict myself, but it is vital, for your emotional wellbeing, that you believe both of these things.

First of all, you are not pathetic. In fact, I'm convinced you have just described every girl you know. We all struggle with our self-esteem and spend time comparing ourselves to others. Nothing can ever be gained from these comparisons – there will always be somebody we deem to be better looking than us, to have a better body or better hair, to be more successful, to have more money, more friends, to be happier and winning at life much more than we are. Believe me, we all do this – girls and boys, men and women. There have been times in my life where I've been torn apart by jealousy, so longing to be like people I follow online that it's consumed my every thought.

The problem with social media is that it doesn't show the whole truth and nothing but the truth. I'm not just talking about filters and Photoshopping and other manipulation to make photos look better, which – believe me – there's tons of. I'm talking about the fact that most of us only ever put our best bits online. I don't usually upload a picture of me without any make-up or when I'm feeling depressed or I've had a rubbish day. I don't post a picture of my dinner if it's turkey dinosaurs and curly fries. I upload a photo of me with my make-up done to perfection, or when I'm at a restaurant eating an impressive dessert. I update my status when I've achieved something, or when I've done something fun, or when I'm with lots of friends. When we compare ourselves to others online, we are comparing our 'behind the scenes' to everyone else's 'highlight reel'. We are assuming that the celebrities, models, bikini bloggers, make-up artists, fitness enthusiasts, etc. only ever live perfect lives. We assume they don't ever have down days, or days when they don't look perfect, or days when they eat curly fries. But they do. Everyone does.

My second point is that, even though we are all part of the same species, we have each grown up in different environments with different people around us, experiencing different things. So everyone – you guessed it – is different.

Try my exercise on page 79 and write down all the things that make you you. This is your manual. Imagine that if an alien came down from space and wanted to know everything about you we could hand them this manual. It's a guide to you – it's what makes you tick.

And if everyone made a manual about themselves, nobody else in the world would have the exact same list as you (unless they copied it). No one will have your exact composition of likes, dislikes, experiences, memories, goals and dreams. Nobody else looks exactly like you and thinks exactly like you. Even if you are a twin, you won't have done everything at exactly the same time, and it's likely you won't have all the same friends. You'll have a different perspective. There has never been anyone else quite like you and there never will be. Once this powerful realisation struck me, I stopped comparing myself to other people. Don't get me wrong, I still get the urge to – we all do – but whenever I find myself looking at another girl and wishing I had her body/hair/life, I remember that we are simply so different we cannot be compared. One person might have a talent for something another person might be rubbish at, but that person will be good at something else instead.

Your boyfriend likes you – that's why he's going out with you. Try not to worry about what he thinks about other girls, because you will never truly know what's going on in his head, and what matters is his actions. Focus on being the girl you want to be and liking yourself, because when we are confident about who we are, people like and fancy us more. You can't control other people's opinions of you – friends, boyfriends, Instagram followers – and you don't have to. The only opinion of you that matters is your own.

Fill out your name in the allotted space on page 64 and tear it out. Stick it on your mirror, on the inside of your wardrobe door or keep it in your purse. Whenever you feel like you're not good enough, repeat the message to yourself: "I AM FIRST NAME SECOND NAME!" You're a brilliant individual and there's no one else like you.

Love,
Katie xxx

THERAPIST SALLY SAYS

It's normal to wonder how we measure up to other people. Some psychologists think this is part of our basic need to understand ourselves and how we fit into the social world. Sometimes other people can really inspire us! But getting too caught up in thinking you are better or worse that someone else is pretty unhelpful.

Images on Instagram don't reveal anything about the complexity of other people's lives – or what's really going on beneath the surface. If we compare our lives to what's on Instagram, we end up setting unrealistic standards for ourselves and imagining that everyone else has it easier or better than we do.

PERFECTIONISM

It's pretty impossible to get everything right all the time, and setting impossibly high standards is usually unhelpful and paralyzing. Perfectionism tends to polarise our thinking – making everything black or white – when the truth is usually in between.

Of course, it's only natural to want to avoid negative feedback like criticism, blame or ridicule – real or imagined, but trying to get things right all the time is really about hiding our own fear and shame.

Some people think that girls are often encouraged to be perfect while boys are allowed to take risks and fail. Give yourself permission to fail, and start aiming for excellence, not perfection – because mistakes are how we learn.

IMPOSTER SYNDROME

Perfectionism can be linked to something called imposter syndrome, where we feel convinced that we're going to be found out for not being good enough or for being a fraud. It feels like everyone knows what they're doing but you. Someone once told me that this feeling comes about because we find it hard to internalize our own achievements. So . . . when you do well at something, make sure you celebrate and get other people to remind you of just how well you've done.

TACKLING PERFECTIONISM

1: **Check your inner voice for negative or catastrophic thinking**

Are you telling yourself things like:

"If I need help from others it means I am weak"

"I can't survive the humiliation of making mistakes"

"I can't let people down"

"I spent all night preparing, but I know I won't do well"

"If I don't get 100% it means I'm a failure"

"What if…."

2: **Be on your guard against perfectionist beliefs – anything that begins with 'should'**

"I should never make mistakes"

"I should never come across as nervous"

"I should always be able to predict problems before they occur"

"I should know the answer"

"I should be able to…"

"I should have…"

3: **Be aware of your perfectionist behaviours – action**

Setting yourself exceptionally high standards
Excessively checking your work, clothes, appearance
Writing impossible to-do lists
Criticising others and yourself

4: **Be aware of your perfectionist behaviours – avoiding action**

Procrastinating
Leaving things to the last minute
Not even trying at all
Hiding from people or situations

5: **Allow yourself to be less than perfect**

Challenge your thinking with some affirmations. Here's a selection, but you could find your own and write them on post-it notes:

- I can only do my best!
- We all learn from our mistakes
- It's OK to get things wrong
- I'm good enough as I am

6: **Be kind to yourself**

What would you advise a friend in the same situation?
What would a friend advise you?

Is there another way to look at this?
Take time for yourself
Let it go

And finally . . . 7: **Compromise**
Give yourself the chance to practise lowering your
own standards. Making mistakes can be frightening for
a perfectionist, so build up slowly and gradually, as if
you were tackling a fear of a physical thing like spiders
or heights.

Remember to ask for help. And don't forget to reward
yourself!

I AM: _____

> "IF YOU JUDGE A FISH ON ITS ABILITY TO CLIMB A TREE, IT WILL LIVE ITS LIFE THINKING IT ISN'T GOOD AT ANYTHING!"

Dear Katie,

I am going to start going to high school soon! I am excited but my one concern is maths. I am in the top set but I am very slow and don't feel confident that I should be in the top set. At my taster days we had maths once. We got given multiplication grids to fill in and I did finish but I was one of the last, which was embarrassing. Please help!

From Me

Hey You,

You say it was embarrassing that you finished last in your test in maths. I have an even more embarrassing maths story – one which I've never told anyone.

My friends and I were messing about and laughing in a maths lesson, and I laughed so hard that I did a little wee on the chair. That hadn't happened to me before. I hadn't wet myself since the early days of primary school when, from what I can remember, it was sort of expected – everyone did it at some point in Reception. But here I was in Year 9, about fourteen years old! When I stood up to leave the lesson some girls noticed the small puddle on my chair. To cover myself, I said, "Ew, I must have sat in something!" but from the looks on their faces they knew what had happened. I've never forgotten that – it's definitely one of the most embarrassing things that's ever happened to me. So it could have been worse. You could have done an accidental wee. OK, random story over, back to maths . . .

I hated maths, not just because I associate the subject with that unfortunate incident, but because I'm more of a words kind of girl. I found it boring and I wasn't good at it.

You've picked up on the fact that your lack of confidence

is part of the problem, which shows your intelligence. I think that was my problem too. I told myself I couldn't do it before I'd even started. I would see equations in front of me and hear everyone else writing away, and I'd sit there in a state of panic.

Don't forget that when you enter a class full of people who are good at maths – guess what? – you are one of those people too! It sounds to me as though you are actually excellent at maths. You are in the top set, which means that working with numbers is one of your strengths. You wouldn't have been put in it otherwise. If you're worried you're falling behind or struggling to keep up, speak to your teacher or ask for some extra support – when I was working towards my GCSEs, I had extra lunchtime sessions with my maths teacher and somehow scraped a B! Both Ms Mayson and I couldn't believe it! It's normal for secondary school to seem very different at first – and it's bound to be a bit more difficult – but it will get easier over time.

As long as you're finishing the work in the allotted time, speed shouldn't be an issue. Perhaps you are slower because you're thinking about the answers properly when others aren't. I'm sure teachers would recommend you take your time. We all work at different paces. If you are working away when everyone has finished, own it. You might think everyone is looking at you and wondering why you haven't finished, but that's probably just in your mind. If anyone is paying attention to what you're doing, maybe they're wondering why they finished so fast, and worrying about their answers! Many people are self-conscious and most likely thinking – and worrying – about themselves more than those around them. For example, I have HUGE handwriting (this book would be twice the size if it was handwritten, and you wouldn't be able to read what it said). When I was in secondary school, I was the ONLY person who had to put my hand up for extra paper in an exam. It was SO embarrassing and I felt really self-conscious. I thought everyone would think I was a super-nerd for writing so much. In reality, I discovered afterwards it had just made my friends concerned that they hadn't written enough! We were all sat in that quiet exam environment feeling awkward and self-aware.

Remember, we're all talented in different ways – we just need to track down what our talents are. It's a clichéd saying, but if you judge a fish on its ability to climb a tree, it will live its life thinking it isn't good at anything! It doesn't matter that you're slower than others at maths. There will be other things you are faster at, and you're still in the top set and doing well academically. Anyway, speedy or not speedy, in the top set or not, even if you were the worst person at maths in the world, it wouldn't matter – you could still live a fulfilling life!

Accept – for now – that you're not going to finish the multiplication grids as quickly as everyone else, and it doesn't matter. Instead, try as hard as you can to pass your exams for whatever future you choose to have. Oh, and remember to always go to the loo before hanging out with your funniest friends.

For anyone who's worrying about maths, whether you're in the top set or it's your worst subject, like it was for me, my brilliant maths teacher from secondary school has offered up her top tips. If I can go from having panicked sweats every time I needed to answer a question to bagging a surprise B in my GCSE, anyone can take on those numbers!

Love,
Katie xxx

TIPS FROM MY SUPER-DUPER MATHS TEACHER,
MS MAYSON!

• Practice makes perfect. This may not be what you want to hear, but the only way to make sure you fully understand a maths concept is by applying it to some problems. The more you practise, the better you will become, which will in turn improve your confidence. Lack of confidence is a major barrier in succeeding in maths, and will make you feel like giving up.

• Understand where you have made a mistake. Going wrong in maths is inevitable. Don't let it deter you from practising. Understanding where and more importantly why you went wrong is your next step to improving. Unpicking your errors is the most powerful way to progress. Working back from a correct answer can be very useful when doing this.

• Create a maths dictionary. Maths has its own vocabulary, which can sometimes be confusing. When coming across a new concept, make a flash card to remind you of it in the future. Include definitions, diagrams and an example with a worked-out solution on the reverse.

> "WHEN YOU DON'T AGREE WITH SOMETHING, ONLY YOU CAN DECIDE IF IT IS GOING TO BE BETTER FOR YOU TO PUSH THE MATTER FURTHER, OR TO GO ALONG WITH THE RULES."

Dear Katie,

I have a question about school.

Why do some schools not allow leggings? My school recently changed the uniform to trousers and we're not allowed to wear leggings anymore. I find it horrible how girls are being taught that clothing is more important than education.

From Me

Hey You,

You're onto something here. It doesn't matter what you're wearing, what matters is what you are thinking, feeling and doing.

My school had similar strict rules about uniform. We weren't allowed little diamanté buckles on our shoes, but these were all the rage when I was in secondary school (please don't think I'm old).

I really didn't see how having a little sparkly buckle on my shoe would affect my education. What was going to happen – would I start staring at my shiny buckle during classes and not pay attention? I was a girl, not a magpie.

What I think is really admirable is that you've questioned the rules. You've asked 'why'. If we didn't question what figures of authority told us from time to time, terribly unjust things would happen in the world. It's not always in your best interests to rebel or kick up a fuss – although sometimes it might be – but there's nothing wrong with questioning why your school has made this particular uniform rule and perhaps suggesting an alternative. I don't know exactly why some schools don't allow leggings. I don't know why your school has changed the rules, but you can ask those in charge to explain it to you.

There might be a good reason for it, or there might not be.

My first job after I left school was working in a shop, which had a warehouse filled with stock at the back. For some reason most of the girls worked on the shop floor serving customers and the boys worked in the back, lugging boxes around. At night, a lorry would come and deliver the stock and a team of boys would unpack the stock and put it onto the shelves. I really wanted to do that job – it was better pay, I liked working in the evenings and it seemed like a laugh. They put their own music on and didn't have to deal with complaints from customers. Together with a female colleague, I mentioned to one of the managers that we'd like the chance to work on the night team, but we were told it was a boy's job. It didn't make sense – it wasn't a strongman competition, the boxes weren't heavy. We were perfectly capable of picking up the boxes and putting them down again in a different place. A few weeks later I had my work 'review' with another manager and was told that I could be perceived as negative because I question the way things are done.

I didn't take the matter any further at the time because I didn't want to lug boxes around that much. I didn't feel it was worth me making a big deal about it, but now I sometimes wonder if I should have done, because what happened was wrong.

When you don't agree with something, only you can decide if it is going to be better for you to push the matter further, or to go along with the rules. Staying true to your own beliefs and questioning rules you don't agree with gives you power, even if you do decide to obey them in order to make life easier for yourself.

You rock, girl. And remember, when you're not in school you can wear whatever you want and be whoever you want to be. Maybe when you grow up you will start a leggings revolution.

Love,
Katie xxx

"LIFE IS ABOUT BALANCE BUT... IT CAN BE TRICKY TO FIND THAT BALANCE"

Dear Katie,

I don't know what to do this summer. I can't get over how bored I am.

From Me

Hey You,

Summer holidays seem to last a lifetime, don't they? I remember being super bored at times because the days stretch out in front of you. At school, you're used to days being filled with a structure. Yes, you sometimes have to do things you don't want to do with your day (get out of bed early, do a lesson you don't like, HOMEWORK!) but now you have too much of that free time and long for a routine to keep you busy.

This is a totally normal feeling. It continues into adulthood. I'm super busy all the time now – as lots of adults are. I'm always working and have little time to fit in my hobbies or relax, but occasionally if I do have some time off, I start to feel bored too – there's only so much sitting around in your PJs you can do. Life is about balance, but because our schedules are dictated by others – we don't choose when we work and go to school – it can be tricky to find that balance.

The good news is that boredom is a state of mind. Some people say that boredom is a lack of imagination. I know that you have an imagination – everybody does – so we have to find yours, and figure out what you can do to have fun.

I'm going to hand this one over to Sally, because she has some brilliant thoughts about boredom.

Love,
Katie xxx

THERAPIST SALLY SAYS

What's the difference between relaxing and being bored?

Relaxation is that feeling of not having to do anything because you are choosing not to. Being bored, on the other hand, is often about feeling like you have nothing to do but it isn't a choice. It's a feeling of being trapped with an excess of thoughts, energy or feelings and the desire to be somewhere else. It's different from relaxing because of the additional energy bubbling around.

The way it makes you feel can be pretty horrible and sometimes that means you switch off, stop concentrating, or find your attention wandering. You can feel like you aren't in control or able to change things, and are being made to do something that you don't want to. It's not surprising that boredom is sometimes a type of anger.

So who would have thought boredom could be a useful thing? Some experts think that being bored is an important part of our survival. Some think it is feeding ground for creativity, and drives us on to do great things.

WHAT MAKES ME, ME!

THINGS THAT ARE BRILLIANT ABOUT ME . . .
e.g. I'm good at talking to people, I like helping people, I have nice eyes!

_____

_____

_____

_____

_____

_____

_____

_____

THINGS I CARE ABOUT AND WANT TO ACHIEVE . . .
e.g. My family, writing a book, passing my exams.

_____

_____

_____

_____

_____

_____

_____

_____

_____

_____

THINGS THAT MAKE ME FEEL GOOD . . .

e.g. Reading, riding my bike, listening to music, learning new stuff, chatting with mates.

_____

_____

_____

_____

_____

_____

_____

"I WOULDN'T WANT LIFE ANY OTHER WAY."

Dear Katie,

I'm really struggling with school. I have so much homework to do and revision for exams, and I'm finding it hard to keep on top of it, and get motivated to actually do the work at home and in school. I've been shouted at a couple of times by teachers recently for not doing my homework, but I don't do one piece of work because I have four others to do and there's no time for all five. It's really stressing me out and I'm not sleeping probably because of it. A couple of my friends feel the same – we are just finding it hard to keep on top of the work.

From Me

Hey You,

Schoolwork, especially at certain times like when you're doing exams, can be all-consuming. When you're older, your work life can be too. I remember being a student working towards my degree, having two jobs, doing a local radio show AND applying for other jobs all at the same time. Then, and whenever work gets on top of me, I try remember to focus on one thing at a time. Even now, sometimes I panic when I start thinking about all the things I have to do and all the work I have coming up. I look at my calendar and want to cry. How can I possibly prepare for so many different work things, write this book, go to the gym, see my friends and family, AND still manage to sleep and eat? The thing is, deep down, I wouldn't want life any other way. I have so many things on my to-do list, because I want to do them. You're worried about schoolwork because you want to do well, otherwise you wouldn't have written to me.

I'm going to answer the rest in a list, because when I write a list I immediately feel clearer about how to tackle things that are overwhelming me!

PRIORITISE
Whenever I get into this panic mode, I ask myself: "What

do you have to do today, Katie? What do you have to do in the next few hours?" And I focus on that first. I want you to try to do the same. Ask yourself what you need to do before tomorrow. What's the first thing you need to focus on? Prioritise your pieces of homework – finish the one that has to be in soonest and then start the next. If we try to do too many things at once we often don't get them done. Tackling them in order will help you feel calmer. That's not to say we can't multi-task a bit too. When I was studying for my exams I would record myself reading out my study notes on my phone, and listen back when I was exercising, travelling on the bus, or tidying my room. I'd stick notes with the information I was struggling to remember all over the walls and read them while I was brushing my teeth or drying my hair – moments when you're not doing anything but a mundane daily task you can do with your eyes closed (might as well have them open and read!).

ASK FOR HELP

Try to chat to a parent or teacher. It's a blessing in disguise that your friends are also finding it all a bit too much – you're not alone. If a group of you chat to your teachers, it may make them want to take action – they might see that you are being a little overworked, and look at amending your schedules to help. Perhaps your teacher could help you put together a timetable, so you can better manage your workload?

REMEMBER EVERYTHING IS TEMPORARY

Remember that this busy spell is temporary and you won't always have to work this hard. Everything will be fine – yes, even if you missed those pieces of homework or failed your exams. Even then! When you've got schoolwork to do, you can either do it with a relaxed, calm and happy attitude, or stress yourself out and waste valuable time feeling unhappy. There's not much point in the latter, is there?

ASK YOURSELF IF YOU REALLY HAVE TO DO IT ALL

Sometimes, I write out my to-do list and then add the words 'or, you could just not do it' after each activity I've planned for myself. It really helps me to realise that it wouldn't be the end of the world if I dropped one of the plates I was spinning.

For example:

KATIE'S TO-DO LIST

- Do your washing
- Tidy your room
- Cut your toenails
- Order a new dress for that party
- Write a chapter of your book

Becomes:

KATIE'S TO-DO LIST
- Do your washing – or, you could just not do it
- Tidy your room – or, you could just not do it
- Cut your toenails – or, you could just not do it
- Write a chapter of your book before the deadline tomorrow – OK, I actually do need to do that one because the deadline is tomorrow, but still, nobody would die if I didn't do it!

You get the picture...

Some of the things I put pressure on myself to do suddenly don't seem so urgent. What's the worst that can happen if I don't tidy my room? Doing this helps me to pinpoint which of the activities I do care about doing – it helps me get my priorities straight.

KEEP A PEN AND PAPER BY YOUR BED

I suffered from insomnia terribly when I was being bullied at school. I had chill-out CDs and pillows smothered in lavender oil, and everything you could possibly think of to help me drift off – but really I needed to refocus my mind. No amount of lavender was going to stop me worrying, and that was what was keeping me awake. I wish I'd realised then that what I needed to do was address my problems head on – in my case the bullying and in yours the schoolwork – and change my perspective on the situation. If you find yourself lying in bed worrying, grab your notepad and write it down. Recording your worries like this helps your mind to 'forget' about them so you can relax.

TURN YOUR PHONE OFF AT NIGHT

Don't use your phone or electronic devices in bed. Read something which isn't too taxing and isn't school-related. This might seem like the craziest, most difficult thing in the world when you've got tons of school stuff to read, but your waking hours will be so much more productive if you sleep well. That said, don't panic about losing sleep either, as this can make it worse – you can't sleep because you worry and then you worry because you can't sleep! I've done twelve hour shifts on live television after having the most terrible night's sleep when I've been nervous or worried. Despite how it feels when you're lying in bed in darkness panicking, you will survive it – you won't fall asleep standing up at the bus stop or simply stop functioning at lunchtime, in fact you won't notice it as much as you think you will, and your body will catch up when it needs to.

Read Radha's tips for a good night's sleep and combatting insomnia when stressed.

It's gonna feel brilliant – if also a little unsettling and weird in a "what do I do now?!" sort of way – when you finally finish your exams! Then you'll spend all summer wondering what to do with yourself! (See page 75 for advice on what to do when you're bored!)

Good luck!

Love,
Katie xxx

DR RADHA SAYS

Sleep is an amazing thing! We tend to think of sleep as a passive time when we aren't doing anything at all, but actually it's the time when our bodies repair themselves, we set down memories in our brains, and hormones that are really important for our body's development are released. So it's important we get enough sleep and we get good quality sleep.

Tips for good sleep:
• Keep your bed a place exclusively for sleeping, so

your brain associates it with sleep, not schoolwork
• Make your bed into a sleep sanctuary with a comfy mattress, pillows and relaxing accessories
• Avoid screens in your room, including your phone
• Make sure your room is dark, quiet and cool. If you can't make your room as dark or as quiet as you'd like because you share a room with a sibling, try using an eye mask or ear plugs
• Go to bed at the same time every night
• Have a pre-bed routine that is always the same, so your brain knows you are getting ready to relax – e.g. take a bath, read a book or listen to calm music

THERAPIST SALLY SAYS

Stress largely falls into two categories:

1: Situations that put us under pressure – when we have too much to do and not enough time – the key here is learning to manage the stuff you need to do.

2: Our reaction to that pressure – how we feel about the things we have to do or things we tell ourselves we have to do. The key here is to develop what psychotherapists call emotional resilience (toughen up a bit) and to know that sometimes it's OK not to feel OK.

Sometimes we just can't change the situation – we have to sit exams, go for that interview, look after a sick relative or juggle lots of things at the same time. The only thing you can do in that case is to take care of yourself and learn how to deal with the situation.

Stress provokes a reaction in the body which usually is seen as our fight/flight/freeze response. If you're stressed you may feel tense, emotional, or overloaded. It feels like life isn't fair and you just can't cope; you may find it hard to make decisions, and get cross with yourself and others. You may be overeating, not sleeping, unable to concentrate, tired, or craving caffeine and sugary things.

STRESS GUIDE
• Drink lots of water
• Get lots of sleep
• Practise deep breathing
• Talk to someone who cares about you
• Meditate with an app (or see our guide on page 128)
• Walk or do some aerobic exercise like running or cycling
• Learn to say no
• Stay off social media for a while
• Be kind to yourself

- See your GP
- Remember that stress is not always a bad thing in itself
– diamonds are formed under pressure.

EXAM STRESS GUIDE
- Ask for extra help if you need to
- Don't compete or compare yourself with your friends
- Eat healthfully
- Exercise when you can
- Don't smoke, drink or take drugs
- Set a schedule
- Establish a revision routine
- Take lots of breaks – maintain a balance between revision and life
- Get into good sleep habits
- Stay away from social media
- Remember: exams are important, but they're not everything

> ## "HUMANS ARE NOT LIKE A MATHS EQUATION – THERE'S NO RIGHT OR WRONG ANSWER ABOUT WHO OR HOW YOU SHOULD BE."

Dear Katie,

I am currently studying for my exams. As is expected, I am very stressed. But my stress is taking over. I no longer feel happy with anything I do. I feel disappointed if I fail to achieve top marks. Crying has become an everyday occurrence in my life – mainly when I am isolated in my bedroom, where no one can hear me, but also in school, during lessons. Teachers have asked me if they can help and they have asked me why I cry. But the truth is that I have no idea . . . Sometimes tears just begin to fall and I can't stop them. I'm sick of feeling sad all the time. I want to be happy. I don't know what's wrong with me and I don't know what to do. I don't feel comfortable talking to my parents about this. The only person I talk to is my friend, but I try not to because I know it makes her sad to see me feeling so low. What should I do?

From Me

Hey You,

I'm so sorry to hear you are feeling like this, and I want you to know that you're not alone. As you say, it is 'expected' that studying for your exams will make you feel stressed, which is infuriating. If everyone expects that, why don't they make 'em less flippin' stressful?

Stress is a natural thing to experience from time to time, but you are right in identifying that your stress has 'taken over'. You say you no longer feel happy with anything you do. I have been there. To me it sounds as though you have low self-esteem, something I have suffered from for as long as I can remember. I know it very well. I suffered with it so badly that it caused me to become depressed.

I used to be insecure about everything about myself. I hated my face, my body, my voice, my TV presenting style. I remember getting incredibly upset with myself when I realised in conversation with friends that I hadn't watched a big TV show they had. What an idiot I was to have missed that experience, I thought. I remember crying because I'd never learned to play an instrument and some people had. What a loser I was, I thought, so I signed up for piano lessons but only had time for about three because I was too busy to fit them in. Every little thing made me feel like the most pointless, rubbish person who had ever existed. I moped about feeling tired – like gravity was pulling me towards the ground stronger than ever before. I felt physically ill – sometimes our minds can make us feel like that. I felt on the verge of crying or screaming all the time. I cried a lot. Sometimes my eyes would fill up with tears when I was on the telly. I don't think anyone noticed – I was good at hiding it. The only person who knew when I'd been crying was my mum. Mummy Thistleton has a special power to always know when I'm upset. She's a witch I think. (Sometimes my dog knew too – dogs are great, aren't they?)

I can't say whether or not you have depression and it's important for you to see a doctor to find out. I went to my doctor, talked to them about the way I was feeling, and was diagnosed with depression. I received treatment for it and soon didn't give a hoot about not having watched that new TV show or not being able to play an instrument or a sport, or not being the best-looking person in the world. I realised that I'm ME. There's no one else like me in the world. I'm good at lots of other things. I'm beautiful for lots of other reasons. I'm not inferior to anyone, and I don't need to try to be – or pretend to be – anything or anyone else. I'll proudly stand up and say "I can't do this" or "I'm not interested in that" without it making me feel less of a person.

You say you don't know why you feel this way. I didn't either. It's not necessarily something specific that makes you want to cry, but an overall feeling of low self-esteem and insecurity that takes over. It can be a whole "I'm just not good enough" thing which casts a dark shadow over us and can get out of hand.

There are so many people who have felt like this. Tennis superstar Serena Williams has talked about how she wanted to be more like her sister growing up and felt inferior to her. Actress Kate Winslet has admitted she was told she didn't have the right look to be an actress, but she persevered despite how insecure this made her feel and went on to prove everyone wrong. *Harry Potter* actress Emma Watson said that she hated how she looked in photos when she was younger because she couldn't match up to how she looked on airbrushed magazine covers. And my absolute hero, J. K. Rowling, has talked about how she suffered from depression when she was a single mother struggling to make ends meet, and how she remembers her 'slowly evaporating sense of self-esteem'. I don't need to tell you how successful she went on to be, but even with that success, she might not be immune to feeling like she isn't good enough. There might be times when she thinks there is room for improvement in her life. See, even celebrities feel like they aren't good enough sometimes.

Some of the most perfect-seeming people have had low self-esteem, just like us. One of the reasons they are so successful might be because striving to be perfect has meant they have worked extremely hard, but lots of them have also reached a point when they've had to be kinder to themselves. They had to realise that there will always be something else you feel you could obtain, or someone you feel is better than you. There is no such thing as a perfect person because our idea of perfect is objective – it's a matter of opinion. Humans are not like a maths equation – there's no right or wrong answer about who or how you should be. Instead of trying to make ourselves better, we should focus on tackling low self-esteem so that we can feel satisfied with who we are.

You can take steps to improve your self-esteem right now and start feeling better right away. Look after this letter for advice from our experts about low self-esteem and depression. And consider going to see a doctor, like I did. I wish I'd done it sooner.

Counselling also helped me. I was given some exercises to help me make sense of things. My counsellors taught me about how the brain works and helped me to realise that my feelings were human – and I just had to stop them from taking over and stealing away all my good feelings. Speaking to a doctor, counsellor or other trusted professional is something I urge you to do. As you say, sometimes it's difficult to chat to those closest to you – either you don't feel comfortable or you don't want to worry them. But I'm glad that you feel you can speak to your friend, and I'm sure they'd rather you confided in them than kept it all inside, regardless of whether it worries them or not. It's likely they feel similar at times, and can sympathise with you.

Check out our guide for dealing with exam stress on page 90. Speak to your teachers and explain how you're feeling, because they will want to help and might be able to suggest a way of adjusting your workload.

You'll find top tips for getting over low self-esteem on the next page. I still have the odd moment when I feel like I'm a right piece of poo, but it doesn't last long, and I'm mostly happy. I only ever cry these days when I watch the John Lewis Christmas advert or see a small dog. And even when I'm not happy, I feel confident that it will pass, that those feelings aren't permanent. They are not who I am. I've survived them before and I will survive them again. And you will too.

Please don't ever feel like you're not good enough. You are. You so so SO are. No matter what grades you get.

Love,
Katie xxx

THERAPIST SALLY SAYS

Self-esteem is how we value ourselves. That self-valuation is based on how we think and feel, so the good news is that we can improve our self-esteem by changing the way we think about ourselves. When we have healthy self-esteem we tend to feel good about ourselves.

But sometimes we're gripped by low self-esteem – the negative opinions which we've formed about ourselves try to fool us into believing they're facts. Low self-esteem can stop us in our tracks and play havoc with our enjoyment of life.

SYMPTOMS OF LOW SELF-ESTEEM
You may feel some of the following:
• Hate or dislike for yourself
• Worthless or not good enough
• Unable to make decisions
• Unable to assert yourself
• Like no one likes you
• Blame for things that aren't your fault
• Unable to recognise your strengths
• Undeserving of happiness
• Low in confidence

TIPS TO KICK START YOUR SELF-ESTEEM
• Stop putting yourself down. If you have a negative thought about yourself – recognise it and do something else, don't get up caught up in it.
• Visualise your inner critic. Give it a name. Then tell it to shut up.
• Challenge your negative thinking, by working out where the beliefs first began and then seeing what experience has shown you about those beliefs. Sit down with your best friend and ask them if they are true.
• Make a list of the positive things in your life

- Start saying no to people you feel are not treating you well
- Even if you don't feel like facing social situations, push through and go – see it as an experiment, and don't worry about getting it perfect
- Take assertiveness training
- Be kind to yourself
- Exercise
- Ask your friends and family to support you

DR RADHA SAYS

Self-esteem is the thoughts and beliefs we choose to think about ourselves, and our opinion of ourselves.

Developing good self-esteem is one of the most important things you can do, because self-esteem is the basis of our mental well-being. It affects how we see ourselves, the world and the others we interact with. Confidence is something that comes from good self-esteem, and once we get those two going we are unstoppable.

Self-esteem, and confidence can go up and down at different times in our lives and it's something all of us have to work on through life. If we have a low opinion of ourselves then we can be at more risk of developing low mood or depression and anxiety long term.

If you need help with your self-esteem, there are lots of things you can try:
• Write a list of all the things you like about yourself (if you find this difficult then ask a sibling or parent or friend to help you). Put this list up on your wall in your room and read it every day
• Look at yourself in the mirror and say something positive about yourself each day, like you would to your best friend
• Practise self-care. Simple things like sleep, exercise, and being kind to yourself can work wonders
• Start a new hobby, to help you increase your confidence and find something you're good at
• Write down a list of the things you think are 'wrong' with you and ask yourself if they are true or not. Ask yourself if there is actual evidence for these things. Is there a more positive way of phrasing your thoughts about yourself?
• Talk to someone about how you feel – it can help to get a more balanced opinion from someone else
If these tips don't work even after trying them for a while or your low self esteem is overwhelming or you feel you may have anxiety or low mood, then go and see your doctor, with your mum or dad or a friend you trust, and ask them for some help.

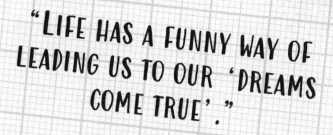

> "LIFE HAS A FUNNY WAY OF LEADING US TO OUR 'DREAMS COME TRUE'."

Dear Katie,

What job should I do in the future?

From Me

Hey You,

You should be a cow farmer.

Or maybe a dentist.

Or actually, how about a circus performer?

"Hang on," you're probably thinking, "I don't like cows or teeth or acrobatics!"

Does it annoy you that someone else is making the decision for you?

I say this because it illustrates the two main points to take into consideration when thinking about what you want to do when you grow up. These are:

1. Do whatever you enjoy doing and what you long to do in your heart.
2. You can always change your mind.

Sometimes when I can't decide between two chocolate bars I flip a coin. If I'm happy with the result then that was clearly the bar I wanted in my heart but if I'm disappointed then I know I wanted the other one – so I choose that. (My heart constantly wants some sort of chocolate.)

Chocolate is a small decision, but whatever it is, big or small, remember that it's YOUR life and YOUR future. Pick the subjects and courses that excite you. They might be the ones you're the best at, or the ones you enjoy the most, or the ones you haven't done before but look like loads of fun. If you enjoy your studies or your job then you'll be passionate about it – you'll work hard, want to do well, be an agreeable person to be around. Those are the qualities which equal a successful person. As we're often good at what we enjoy, we can turn these things into our careers. We humans have this idea that work is something we should dread, that it shouldn't be enjoyable – after all, it's called WORK. That's not true. I have hard and tiring days at work, but I don't dread Mondays – I love what I do.

Sometimes it's something that's hindered you or been seen as a flaw that's the key to your future. I have met voice-over artists who used to get detention for doing impressions of their teachers, and TV directors who got told they watched too much TV. I used to get told off for talking too much, and I could never stick to a word limit when writing an essay or story. I now talk and write for a living. So think about what you are best at and enjoy every day. You can turn any of your hobbies or interests into a career – reading (maybe you'll be a book editor), debating (maybe you'll be a lawyer), party planning (you could work in events), crosswords (maybe you're a born codebreaker), number puzzles (a genius mathematician), stargazing (are you a budding astronaut?), drawing buildings (maybe you'll be an architect), looking after people (nursing, perhaps?). Maybe you're brilliant at chatting, which could make you great in PR, or presenting! The list goes on...

What makes you tick? What job would feel the least like work to you? Sometimes I can't believe I'm paid to mess around on the telly. I've had to work hard to get there, but it was worth it.

The other point to remember is that you don't have to decide on everything right now. If people keep asking what you want to do when you grow up (people can be so annoying, can't they?), just say "I'm not sure yet – but next I'm planning on doing [insert thing you're gonna do next here], because I really enjoy it."

When I was your age I wanted to be a writer – and right now I am sitting here writing my first book. But I've had other jobs, and the path hasn't been as simple as I thought. Still, that path has been even more fun than I'd imagined. While I've always wanted to write books, I also decided during university that I wanted to be a journalist. Then as I trained to be a newspaper journalist I decided I wanted to be a radio presenter, and while working as a radio presenter, I got a job at the BBC . . . The point being, it's amazing how many jobs you discover that you didn't even know existed, once you enter the working world – jobs right up your street. I was given the opportunity to be a TV presenter – something which had never even crossed my mind. It was a terrifying first couple of years, but I grew to love the job and

wouldn't have it any other way now. What's more, my job as a TV presenter has given me amazing opportunities to write – for radio, TV, and now for this book. These are opportunities I might have missed if I hadn't gone down a path I didn't plan. Life has a funny way of leading us to our 'dreams come true'.

It's not always easy to decide what we want to spend the rest of our lives doing, but despite what we are sometimes led to believe, we don't have to decide the rest of our lives right now. Lots of people aren't sure what they want to do in the future when they're in school, and many people still don't know when they're at university. Some people who did know, then change their minds a few years into their career, and start again from scratch. We're can always change our minds – it can take a while to figure out who we are and what type of lifestyle suits us. And different things can be right for us at different times. Every class you take, every course you complete, qualification you acquire, person you meet, hobby you try and skill you learn is going to enrich your life and teach you so much.

Everything we do helps us in our future jobs and lives, even if we don't realise it at the time. The skills we pick up from our different experiences aren't always obvious, but they are there, and they make us who we are.

What an exciting time this is for you. Take a deep breath and remember to enjoy it – 'the chase' is often the best bit.

Love,
Katie xxx

> "THERE WILL BE GOOD TIMES AND BAD TIMES, JUST LIKE THERE ALWAYS ARE IN LIFE, BUT YOU WILL SURVIVE, AND ENJOY IT TOO."

Dear Katie,

I am nervous for when we move on to high school and university and we split up from all of our friends, and start to do exams and studies. We might not find new friends, and get low marks on exams, and have loads of homework. What are your tips?

From Me

Hey You,

I remember in secondary school when we had to have an immunisation jab, which was one injection in your arm and a little tablet on your tongue that sort of fizzed away. It was the stuff of legend – in a bad way. As we queued up in alphabetical order, the As and Bs of the year couldn't wait to tell the rest of us how awful it was.

"IT FEELS LIKE A FLY GOING INTO YOUR MOUTH AND VOMITING ON YOUR TONGUE," one person said. "IT HURTS WELL MORE THAN THE TB!" said someone else, referring to the tuberculosis jab we'd had the year before.

I approached the front of the queue, trembling and wondering if the nurses grew tired as the time went on, and became more aggressive with the needle as a result. I watched people freak each other out, and the odd person cry as they held their arm. When it came to my turn, I braced myself and shut my eyes, so I practically missed the entire event. Both the injection and tongue-tablet had been nothing to worry about at all.

People like to tell scary stories and make life events sound so much more terrifying than they actually are. "EXAMS ARE SO HARD!" we cry, "JOB INTERVIEWS ARE SO SCARY!" "HAVE YOU KISSED A BOY/GIRL YET? FIRST KISSES ARE A MASSIVE DEAL! YOU BETTER DO IT RIGHT!"

The move to secondary school is one of these things. I'm not denying that it's a big change in your life, because it is. I'm also not saying you shouldn't find it hard to deal with, or struggle with friendships or exams or homework, because you might, and you should seek help and advice if you do. But it won't necessarily be all doom and gloom, and most likely it will be easier to cope with than you're imagining, so don't fret too much about something you haven't encountered yet. Worrying about problems we-don't-actually-have-yet-but-might-have-one-day is such a waste of feeling content and comfortable. That's not to say we don't all do it, and find that feeling hard to fight sometimes.

It's understandable to feel nervous about moving on to secondary school, and then university, but let's hold our horses for a second. If you haven't yet started secondary school, university is SO far away that it certainly isn't worth worrying about now. By the time you get to that stage – if you decide you want to go to university – you will be such a further-education whizz, you'll be like "I've got this". You'll have grown and changed as a person – so let's cross that bridge when we come to it. When I first started secondary school I remember thinking, "THIS PLACE IS MASSIVE." I couldn't comprehend the size of it compared to my teeny tiny primary school. One vivid memory I have from starting secondary school is falling over. Not just once – my best friend Mel and I used to fall over all the time. We were like Bambi on ice. It was as if we'd been given a special new pair of secondary school legs that we hadn't learned to use yet. In reality, it was all to do with us rushing around – we were so concerned we'd be late for a class or miss the school bus. We'd never had to get public transport without grown-ups before.

Most of us feel overwhelmed when we move from primary to secondary. You've worked hard for years to feel confident and accepted and safe and know the school inside out. You feel like the absolute boss – you're the oldest and most respected kids in the whole school! Then all of a sudden, as if someone has pulled a rug from underneath your feet, you're back to square one. You're the newbie who doesn't know anyone or know your way around.

But as quickly as these new, nervous feelings and situations come along, they disappear again. Within a week or two you'll begin to get your bearings, and the school won't seem so big any more. (And by the time you leave you will think it's teeny tiny, like your old primary school.) Making friends seems daunting, but everyone is in the same situation. Many others will be worried about making friends too; people will want to talk to you and become your mate. You will get lots of homework I'm sure, but I'm also sure you'll be given guidance so you can complete it. You will do exams, and you will find some of them easy and others difficult, but you can get help with the ones you're struggling with. Your teachers want you to pass exams – their jobs depend on it. So while it seems big and scary now when you look ahead, that's just because you're not there yet. You will grow along with it. You will get older and smarter and able to take on more responsibilities – it's part of the gradual process of growing up. You won't all of a sudden be expected to do something you're not prepared for.

You will also have so much fun. Some of the best times I've ever had were at secondary school with my friends. There will be good times and bad times, just like there always are in life, but you will survive, and enjoy it too. Here are some of my top tips for those first couple of weeks. Hopefully after the first month you'll have settled right in, and next year you'll see the new kids starting from primary school, just like you a year ago. You'll remember that nervous feeling which now feels so far away and perhaps you'll have the opportunity to be kind, help them out, and make their first days as good as yours were.

TIPS FOR STARTING SECONDARY SCHOOL:
• Get to class early and chat to the first person you see. I used this tactic at college and university – it's my magic 'friend-making' trick and it really works. Read the advice

I gave on page 180 about making friends, as that will also be helpful.

• Be nice to everyone and stay out of dramatic situations. Trust me – life is much easier this way. Try not to fall out with friends on social media – switch it off, if you can see things going that way. With all those hormones flying around, secondary school friendships can be intense sometimes, but if you're nice to everyone you'll always come out on top.

• Do your homework as soon as you get home. The school day will be fresh in your mind, making the homework much easier. Once it's done you can enjoy yourself and avoid the dread of a deadline looming over you. I used to spend an hour getting my homework done before I met my friends or watched any TV, almost like an extended hour of school (yawn). It stops homework feeling like it's taking up too much of your actual 'home' time. After that you can see friends, eat, watch telly and let your brain cells turn to mush for the evening.

• Try not to skip any classes or be late, because missing stuff will make exams more difficult. If you have to miss something, ask your teacher what you can do to catch up. Absorbing information slowly throughout the year works much better than 'cramming' right before exams (although we're all guilty of doing a bit of that, myself included!).

• If you're struggling in any lessons, ask your teacher to recommend books, lunchtime or after-school clubs or tutoring sessions that might help. It will take a weight off your shoulders if you're doing all you can to get the grades you deserve.

• Enjoy yourself! There can be a lot of pressure put on secondary school students to get good grades and do piles of homework, but what's most important throughout your teenage years is your happiness. If you failed every single one of your exams, you'd still survive and be able to pick yourself up and start again. Secondary school can feel like the 'be all and end all', but when you leave, you no longer have to do the subjects you don't like or see any of the people you're not so keen on! Take these next few years to figure out what makes you happy – get some hobbies, build friendships and find your favourite subjects, so you can put your own emotional health and happiness first.

Take deep breaths, straighten out your tie and smile as you walk into secondary school on your first day. Until then, shake off any worrying thoughts that creep into your head. This is an exciting time and sometimes we can't decipher whether those butterflies in our tummy are of excitement or nervousness! But focus on the positives – think about all the good things that are going to happen to you in the next few years – instead of the negatives. You're going to be OK, no matter what happens.

Love,

Katie xxx

THERAPIST SALLY SAYS

Change can be wonderful and inspiring, but it also can make us feel anxious, off balance, lonely and a bit sad, especially if we haven't chosen it.

But when you think about it, everything that's alive is changing all the time. Nothing stands still and we all have to cope with change every day – even when we don't realise it's happening.

Give yourself time. If you can, find someone to talk with about what you miss or are finding hard to get used to. Remember that sometimes anticipating changes can be scarier than going through the changes themselves. Charles Darwin, who knew a thing or two about survival, thought that learning to adapt was one of the most vital human skills. So see any change as good practice!

TIPS FOR COPING WITH CHANGE:
• Accept that the change has happened, and go with the flow
• Give yourself permission to be a bit emotional and vulnerable
• Be kind to yourself
• Ask for help
• Find somewhere/someone safe to let off steam about

how you're feeling
- Get comfortable with saying "I don't know"
- Know that you're not on your own
- Keep to a routine
- Realise that sometimes even good change can be stressful
- Exercise and eat healthfully
- Write down all the positives that come from this change
- Work out where you are in the cycle of change (letting go of the old, cooking the new, actually dealing with the new phase)

If you find yourself becoming anxious, focus on your breathing and look at our anxiety guide on page 123.

NOTES

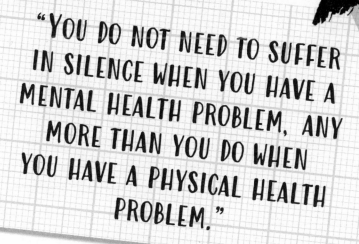

"YOU DO NOT NEED TO SUFFER IN SILENCE WHEN YOU HAVE A MENTAL HEALTH PROBLEM, ANY MORE THAN YOU DO WHEN YOU HAVE A PHYSICAL HEALTH PROBLEM."

Dear Katie,

I struggle with anxiety and now it's turning into health anxiety (hypochondria) and it's driving me crazy! People think I'm just over-exaggerating when I say I worry I have a brain tumour. It would feel amazing to know I'm not alone. And it's weird because my anxiety happens at night. I still worry about my health throughout the day, but it's worse at night and that is when I have panic attacks. I would LOVE to know how to slow my breathing down and how to control them.

From Me

Hey You,

You say you'd feel amazing to know you're not alone –
well, I can tell you with complete confidence that you are
100% not alone! Anxiety is a hugely common problem
and tons of people suffer from it. In fact, I bet lots of
people you know have it without you realising. I have
suffered with anxiety all my life. I started becoming aware
of it when I was about your age, although sometimes I
wonder if it started much earlier, as I used to struggle
with taking deep breaths and always had sweaty hands
when I was a young child! The asthma tests I had when I
was a teenager showed my lungs were absolutely fine – I
only realised as I grew older that I'd been suffering from
panic attacks all along. For years I'd wondered what was
wrong with me, but had never thought about my mental
health – I'd been too busy worrying that it was a physical
problem.

Like you, I always worried at night, and that's common
too. Has anyone ever said to you, "It will all seem
better in the morning?" It often does, doesn't it? There's
something about the night-time – the darkness, the quiet
– which makes you worry about terrible things which
probably won't happen to you. Worrying is a perfectly
normal feeling – we worry in order to protect and look
after ourselves. We worry about our health so that we
spot anything that might be wrong early – but while it's

important that we 'worry' enough to make sure we stay healthy, ideally we stop worrying before the worrying itself harms our health!

A panic attack isn't going to kill you. Try to remember that in those moments when you're breathing super-fast but it feels like you're not really taking any air in, when your heart feels like it will explode, when you think you're going to die.

That won't happen. When your breathing gets out of control, try to push the physical symptoms out of your mind, reminding yourself that they aren't real. The problem is in your mind, and it is manifesting itself with physical symptoms.

Some people suggest taking slow, deep breaths in and out to combat panic attacks. I didn't find this worked for me, because it made me concentrate on my breathing even more, and I'd end up in a cycle of panicking about my breathing. But it might work for you.

What works for me is making like Taylor Swift and simply shaking it off when I feel a panic attack creeping towards me. I literally shake my head and say to myself, "Oh, don't let your mind start doing that to your body," and focus my thoughts on something else instead. I find focusing on my feet extremely effective. Look down at your feet, press them to the floor, remind yourself that you are here in the moment, standing on your two feet, and that everything is fine. Try really feeling your feet touching the floor by wiggling each toe in turn, starting with the big toe and ending with the little one (some are harder to wiggle than others!). Really feeling the sensation of your heels pressing into the ground can help get you back to the right now, rather than worrying about what may be.

Some people find keeping a rubber band on their wrist helpful, which they play with when they feel anxious, to distract them from sliding into a panic attack. Another method is to make a list of everyday things, such as what colour socks you have in your drawer, or the contents of your pencil case. Different things work for different people, so experiment to find out what works for you – the worst that can happen is that it doesn't work, in which case you can try something else next time.

Now you know that what you're feeling is not physically harming you, and you have some techniques to try when you feel yourself starting to panic, it's important to figure out what's causing the panic attacks in the first place. Dealing with that should reduce the amount of anxiety you have – then we've nailed it!

I have always suffered from generalised anxiety disorder

– I'm anxious about things very frequently, such as education, work, reputation, appearance and family. I worry that I won't have any money, or my close relatives will die, or that the people I just socialised with will think I was weird, or boring, or ugly. I care too much about what people think and I'm often on edge – jittery and fidgeting and rushing around, with my breathing at 100 miles per hour. I've accepted that this is who I am – and in many ways it's a good thing. It's the reason I'm motivated and ambitious and caring. I'm sure you have many characteristics which people love and respect about you that you wouldn't have if you weren't a big worrier – so let's embrace anxiety as one of our traits and celebrate it. It doesn't make you weird or a bad person!

So, on to identifying the cause of your anxiety. The first question to ask is: has there been a time when you've worried about something that hasn't happened?

Has there been a time when you've worried about something and it has happened – but you survived anyway?

Your anxiety is primarily focused on health issues. I'm assuming, as you don't mention any, that you don't have any particular reasons to worry about your physical health.

Let's imagine you're a scientist and you are testing
two different hypotheses to find out which one is true:
hypothesis A or hypothesis B.

Hypothesis A is that you have a serious health condition,
even though there isn't any evidence for one.

Hypothesis B is that you don't have a serious health
condition, and it's actually your brain messing with you
and telling you to think this. You already know that
you are suffering from anxiety and hypochondria.

You have evidence to support hypothesis B, but nothing to
support A, which means that scientist-you will choose B
as the truth.

There's a flow chart after this letter, which I put together to
use as a formula for whenever I worry about something. I
find it works for me, and I hope it does for you too.

While trying my suggestions, please also remember
that anxiety is a health problem too – you can see your
doctor about it if you're struggling to cope. You do
not need to suffer in silence when you have a mental
health problem, any more than you do when you have
a physical health problem. I wish I'd sought help sooner
than I did. Now I've accepted that I have anxiety, and use
the flow chart to put my worries into perspective and think

about them rationally, my panic attacks are few and far between. I enjoy getting into my cosy bed ready for a good night's sleep, instead of dreading the panic that used to lie ahead!

Sleep soundly, and well done for being a worrier – it means you have a zest for life.

Love,
Katie xxx

DR RADHA SAYS

Anxiety is a feeling we get, related to fear. When we are frightened of something, we worry and then feel anxious. When we think a situation is a threat, our body's sympathetic nervous system is activated and produces a hormone called adrenaline. This response is called 'fight or flight'. We are either supposed to fight the threat or run away, so we need more blood supply to go to our muscles and around our bodies. Adrenaline causes our heart rate to increase and our blood pressure to go up, and our breathing gets shallow and fast in order to run or fight.

Panic attacks are acute and intense episodes of this

process, and they can sometimes occur out of nowhere. At other times there can be a specific trigger like a phobia or a thought you find distressing. Panic attacks can last for anywhere between five and thirty minutes and can be extremely distressing and frightening. You can get a dry mouth, breathlessness and disorientation, sweating and a feeling like your heart is racing. People often say it feels like they are going to die.

Luckily, there are things you can do to help control your panic attacks and to reduce how often they happen.

WHAT TO DO WHEN YOU ARE HAVING A PANIC ATTACK:
• Try to focus on your physical surroundings and put your attention on something you can see or feel
• Say to yourself 'this is a panic attack and it will pass'. Sometimes people have this or something similar written down on a bit of paper or their phone, that they can read
• Breathing exercises – breathe in slowly through your nose and out of your mouth and count as you breathe. Some people find it helpful to count for five in and five out. Keep doing this to slow your breathing down. This activates the parasympathetic nervous system, which is the 'brake' system in a panic attack
• It is helpful to have someone you trust who you

can contact or be with to reassure you that it will pass and you are safe

WHAT TO DO TO HELP REDUCE THE FREQUENCY OF PANIC ATTACKS:
• Talking therapies – including cognitive behavioural therapy (CBT) – can be really useful and effective for changing the thought patterns that can trigger panic attacks
• Exercising, eating regularly and sleeping well can help
• Practising breathing exercises every day
• Meditation or mindfulness
• Avoiding caffeine, smoking and alcohol
• Understanding what a panic attack is and knowing that the feelings will pass

THERAPIST SALLY SAYS

Anxiety is a form of extreme stress. Anxiety is usually caused by what we imagine might happen – worrying about things going wrong or feeling like we're in some kind of danger.

Anxiety is a natural human reaction, and is part of our

human survival system – it kicks in whenever we sense danger or a threat. Our body releases adrenaline to help us to get out of the situation quickly. Some anxiety is good, but it can take over physically, emotionally, and change the way we see the world. The problem is that our brain doesn't always know the difference between a real threat and something we're just really worried about, so our brain can kick off a series of chemical responses as if our life is in danger when it's really not.

The extra adrenaline released into our body increases our heartbeat, making it hard to breathe. We get sweaty, our hands and feet can shake and we feel dizzy. Our thoughts race and we begin to imagine catastrophes. We might think negative thoughts or even not sleep.

The symptoms of a panic attack are real but they're not caused by a physical illness – it's caused by your body releasing lots of adrenaline to help with your flight/fright/freeze response – a survival tool that dates back thousands of years. The feelings, thoughts and sensations always pass eventually, but at the time you feel out of control.

There's the panic attack and then also panic about the panic attack. Sometimes you catch yourself going into a panic attack and that can trigger even more panic. If you catch yourself panicking, try the breathing exercises below. It can also help to focus on one thing, pouring all your attention to how a stone looks or how a clock sounds, for example. Doing breathing exercises every day can help you prevent panic attacks and they can help when a panic attack occurs. You may feel tired afterwards, as the adrenaline drains from your body. If you feel like anxiety is taking over then it's important to talk to someone. CBT therapy can help, so see your GP. See our mindfulness guide below.

MINDFULNESS GUIDE

I'm a big fan of mindfulness – it's one of the best ways I know of to help with stress. Mindfulness is all about being in the present, without judging anything. Instead of getting caught up in thinking about stuff in the past or the future, mindfulness is being aware of what's going on right now and being kind and curious about it.

The best thing about mindfulness is that you can do it anywhere, anytime, because it's all about breathing, noticing what's happening and then letting it go. It sounds simple, but it's not always easy to do, especially when you are stressed! It's good to practise every day if you can – even if it's only for a few minutes.

HERE ARE SOME EXERCISES TO TRY:
5-MINUTE BREATHING EXERCISE

• Focus on your breathing. If you can, shut your eyes too.

• Breathe in slowly, deeply and gently through your nose, trying to breathe into your belly, not your chest.

• Breathe out slowly, deeply and gently through your mouth.

• Repeat this breath three times.

• Then breathe in slowly, deeply and gently through your nose.

• Breathe out slowly, deeply and gently through your nose.

• Repeat this breath three times.

• It can help to count steadily from one to five on each in-breath and each out-breath.

• Each time your attention wanders, just bring your focus back to the breath.

3-MINUTE SENSES EXERCISE

• Notice what you are experiencing right now through your senses.

• Take a few slow breaths. Really pay attention to one thing and become a witness to the present moment:

• What do you hear? (e.g. ticking clock, your breath, wind blowing, traffic)

• What do you see? (e.g. picture, chair, dog, phone, glass of water)

• What do you feel? (e.g. the chair you're sitting on, the ground under your feet, warm, cold)

• Focus on one of these things and each time your attention wanders, bring your focus back to the sound or thing you're looking at or feeling.

KATIE'S WORRY FLOW CHART

How to deal with a problem you can't get off your mind!
If you're worrying about something in particular, try this flow chart and see if it makes you feel better. I made this when I was suffering from anxiety and I find it works when I apply most of my fears and concerns to it. I hope it helps you too!
I have used 'struggling with schoolwork' as an example problem here, but you can apply it to whatever you're worrying about. It may help to grab a pen and paper to write down your own notes as you go along.

STEP 1 – WHAT I'M FEELING IS HUMAN
First, accept that whatever emotion your feeling is human. It's there for a reason. Worries are human nature and there to protect us, but sometimes we're not very good at filtering out the worries we don't need to spend a lot of time on. Think about why you feel like you do and say it out loud.

For example: "I'm feeling really worried about my schoolwork, which is because I want to impress my family and I don't want to look stupid. I feel this way because, as a human being, I care about being able to provide for myself, I care about what my family and friends think of me and I care about my future."

↓

STEP 2 – HOW DO I WANT TO FEEL?
Think about how you want to feel. This is the fun part. Don't hold back – think about exactly how you would want to feel in an ideal world, no matter how unrealistic.

For example, "I want to feel like I am completely competent at school, and that I'm never going to fail. I want to know that my exam results are going to be brilliant, so that I can stop worrying about them."

STEP 3 – WHAT CAN I DO TO CHANGE MY SITUATION?
Now think about what action you can physically take to get closer to how you want to feel. You might need to 'get real' a bit here.

For example, you can't find out what your future exam results will be, or know that you're never going to fail. You can't be completely competent at school either – nobody is. But what can you do? You can speak to your teacher, and do some extra classes or have some tutoring. You can tell your parent or guardian, and see if you can perhaps move classes, change exam papers or get hold of some extra books which might help. Write down the action you CAN realistically take. Sometimes there isn't one. We can't always change our situation – step 4 will help with this.

STEP 4 – ACCEPTING MY SITUATION AND CHANGING MY PERSPECTIVE

Something else you can do – and this is an important bit – is try to change the way you're viewing the problem. Like I said earlier, you can't find out for sure what your future exam results will be. It would be great if you could – you wouldn't need to worry at all! But we don't have special powers or a crystal ball, what we do have is the ability to change our perception of the problem.

Some people were born geniuses. Some people were not. Some people were born with health problems, and some were born with excellent genes. Some people were born into rich families, and some into poor.

We are all different, and we all have a different set of circumstances. There is no perfect person, or perfect life. Whatever you are going through does not need to take away all your happiness – you can make the best of any situation.

For example, you can accept that you are not finding schoolwork as easy as you'd like to, or as easy as others might be finding it. That is who you are. Say it out loud: "I have to work a lot harder than some people to get a good grade." Does your problem sound so bad once you've aired it, and accepted it? Can you be happy regardless and make the best of your life? I'm sure you can. Whatever you are worrying about will not be the end of your world.

STEP 5 – TALKING TO SOMEONE

Another thing that can be helpful is to talk to someone about what you're worrying about. No matter how silly you think it might sound, chances are they will have worried about something similar. If there's no one to talk to right away, write your problem down. Imagine you are advising a friend – what would you suggest they do if they approached you with this concern? Be your own agony aunt.

STEP 6 – FOCUSING ON WHAT MATTERS TO ME

Focus on what matters to you and what makes you happy. Make a list of everything you really care about and enjoy doing – everything that makes you feel good. Is the thing you are worrying about going to change the course of your life? Probably not. Focus on doing things that make you happy, and things that matter to you. There are lots of different aspects to your life. If one is getting you down, spending more time on another will remind you that there are many things to be positive about, even if you're going through a tough time.

For example, say to yourself: "I am struggling with a particular subject at school, so I'm going to take action and do some extra classes to improve as much as I can. I am also going to remember other things that matter – my family and enjoying my hobbies – and spend time focusing on those things as well. Every time you start worrying, busy yourself doing something you enjoy and care about.

NOTES

"DON'T TURN AGAINST YOURSELF. BE YOUR OWN BEST FRIEND."

Dear Katie,

I'm thirteen years old. I have been unhappy with the way I look since I was ten. Everyone looks so pretty. I look like a potato. When I was eleven I got bullied by this girl. She'd shout at me for no reason. I told my teachers and parents but they thought I was joking and making a mountain out of a molehill. I then got bullied continually by two girls and some of the boys in year eight. It was horrible. One boy called me an 'ugly rat' online. I didn't like who I was. I still don't now. I need your help – what should I do?

From Me

Hey You,

Let's compartmentalise some of these thoughts you are having, and deal with them one at a time.

• You sound very unhappy with how you look. I am so sorry to hear that. It makes me sad to hear that people your age are struggling with their perceptions of their own appearance. You're not the only one going through this and not the only one to write to me about it. I haven't ever seen a human being who looks like a potato – I can guarantee you don't! But most people feel like this from time to time. Even those who you say 'look so pretty' will feel like this. To them, they won't look so pretty. You think you look like a potato, others will wish they looked like you. These problems aren't physical or anything to do with the way we look – they are in our minds. Luckily there are steps we can take to feel better and build our confidence and self-esteem.

• Don't tell yourself you are ugly or look like a potato. Lots of us are guilty of speaking to ourselves in this way. Sometimes I call myself terrible names in my head, because I've scoffed a slice of cake. We don't realise that allowing these thoughts can damage our own self-esteem over time – we are effectively bullying ourselves! This is how bullying works – you repeatedly tell somebody they are not good enough until they believe it. Have you noticed how many times we put ourselves down just in one day? If someone compliments my dress, I say, "Oh, this old thing, it's really cheap/old/creased." If someone says I look "well", I say, "No chance! I've been eating like a pig/I'm really tired/I'm covered in spots/I rushed my hair today." What is wrong with just saying thanks and feeling good about the compliment we've received? Do we do this because we are modest and don't want to come across as arrogant? Or do we do it because we are our own worst critics and have insulted ourselves so many times that we've started to believe it?

• Let's reverse this. Write down a list of all of the brilliant things about you. (You can use the allotted space on page 79.) Not just your physical attributes – that you have nice eyes, soft skin, thick hair etc. – but some of your other qualities too. We are much more than our outer shell. Our personalities are what make us good looking – they ooze out of us in our mannerisms, our body language, our facial expressions and our speech!

• Try not to let what anybody else says about you affect how you feel about yourself. Now that I have grown up and dealt with my issues with my appearance, I no longer think I am ugly. Let me be clear: I don't think anyone is. I have learned about beauty – I've met people, travelled, read, watched TV, and become educated about how beauty is defined. Do you know that a vlogger once sent her picture to lots of countries and asked each one to 'make her beautiful'? People around the world used computer technology to edit her picture and the results were fascinating – each country had a completely different idea of what beauty was. Beauty is objective and different people find different traits beautiful.

• Take up a hobby to build your confidence. This can be daunting, but when I was your age I started a drama class to make me feel better about myself. You could do something like that, or perhaps something sporty. Exercise releases endorphins and will help to make you feel great about how you look, as well as giving you a sense of achievement and improving your health. Drama class enables you to talk in front of groups of people, make new friends and improves your overall confidence. Becoming good at something new also gives you a satisfaction which can take the focus off worrying about how you look. Whenever I feel rubbish about how I look I remind myself of all of the non-appearance-based skills I have, like being able to present live telly or radio, and making a great apple crumble. If you're scared about joining a new class, ask your parents to help you find one where you won't know anyone. This can be less scary as you don't have anything to lose! Feeling embarrassed in front of strangers isn't half as bad as feeling embarrassed in front of people you know. You might find you make some new friends and start feeling better about yourself.

• Now, let's talk about the bullying. Consider speaking to your parents and teachers again, if this is still continuing. Make it clear to them that you are not over-exaggerating – bullying needs to be stopped in its tracks. They might not want to admit to themselves that you are having problems. I don't know why they haven't realised it is hurting you. Perhaps to them it doesn't seem like what the people in question are doing is a big deal, perhaps the boys and girls who are bullying you don't realise they are doing it – that doesn't matter – because to you it is a big deal, it is hurting you. Sometimes people hurt others without realising it. Be clear with your parents and teachers about how you feel. You could try finding a different teacher to chat to about it, or another adult you trust – a grandparent, older sibling or friend's parent maybe? Schools need to be aware that bullying is taking place in their environment, and it's their responsibility to help you to stop feeling like this. Of course online bullying often happens outside the school gates, and can be worse because people are often even nastier when they can hide behind their computer screens. It's likely that these people are being mean because they are suffering too. Block anyone who makes you feel bad. Try taking a break from your social media accounts and see if this helps both the bullying and your confidence. Social

media can be very bad for us if we spend too much time on it and allow it to influence our thoughts.
Have a look at my social media rules on page 206 for more information.

Don't turn against yourself. Be your own best friend. You have the power to make yourself as happy as possible. You owe it to your brilliant self!

Love,
Katie xxx

> "HELP IS ALWAYS AVAILABLE TO US, WHATEVER WE MIGHT BE GOING THROUGH. WE DON'T NEED TO FIGHT OUR MINDS ON OUR OWN."

Dear Katie,

This isn't a question. I wanted to contribute something so that I could maybe help people who are going through the same things as I am, as I know I am not the only person battling schizophrenia.

I was only diagnosed last year, after an episode at school which involved my teachers having to help me. I was treated in hospital. I'm on my way to 'recovery' now. Schizophrenia is a thing that will always be a part of me and I've got to try to adjust, but things are going well.

It's a very hard thing to come to terms with and a lot to take in – people often think I am a 'crazy person'. I just want to raise awareness and I want people to know they're not alone and you can adjust, but it will take time. I want children and teens to understand that no matter what, they can always ask for help, because people care, they really do.

I hope this helps to shed a bit of awareness and understanding.

From Me

Hey You,

Schizophrenia can be a very scary illness, and I'm glad you say things are going well for you.

You are right to want to raise awareness – this is an illness like any other, and sometimes we forget that mental illnesses are not our fault, just like physical illnesses aren't either. You're right, you are not a 'crazy person', you are a person with an illness who needed help, got help, and is now starting to feel better.

What you've learned is that help is always available to us, whatever we might be going through. We don't need to fight our minds on our own – if we're feeling unwell in our mind, we can speak to a doctor or therapist, just as we would if we felt physically unwell. And as you've learned, doing this can help to massively improve your life.

You don't need to tell people about your illness if you don't want to – it's your business. You also don't need to hide it, as it's nothing to be ashamed of. I agree that we need to greatly increase awareness of this sort of problem, so that we can better understand what others, and ourselves, might be going through. Do what feels right for you. Do what makes you feel better. You're going to have the brilliant life you deserve, now that you've got help for your illness – there's nothing it should stop you from doing.

Your teachers are aware of your illness and sound like they have been supportive so far – could they teach your fellow students about it? Could they introduce some lessons on mental health, with the aim of helping others who may be in your situation, and also help people to understand you and what you're going through?

I think you're a wonderful person for writing to me and wanting to spread awareness through my book. Thank you – both on my behalf and the people you will have helped. I've asked Radha and Sally to provide some info about mental illnesses below, to educate those reading who are curious to know more, and to help you on your mission to show young people that they are not alone, and that there is always help available.

I wish you well on your road to recovery, you brilliant person.

Let's keep fighting the mental health stigma together.

Love,
Katie xxx

DR RADHA SAYS

Schizophrenia is a mental health condition. It's a form of psychosis which means people interpret things or see things around them that are not based in reality. It can cause a person to have hallucinations (seeing or hearing things that are not there), delusions (beliefs that are not based in reality and are unusual), changes in behaviour and confused thoughts. It can also cause people to isolate themselves or sometimes to have low motivation. We don't fully understand why it happens but we think there could be higher risk of developing schizophrenia from our genetics, chemical changes in our brains, stressful life events or structural changes in our brains.

Just like with physical health conditions, the most important thing you can do as a friend to someone with schizophrenia or any mental health condition is to try and understand and be there for them. Supporting them is one of the best things we can all do to help them get better, stay well and cope with ups or downs. It is also really great to read about mental health conditions, to give us the knowledge we need to help others.

If you are experiencing symptoms that are worrying you or you notice changes in a friend, then get some support from your GP straight away. There are some very effective treatments and some excellent charities and support groups.

THERAPIST SALLY SAYS

We all go through phases of feeling anxious, angry, depressed, different, wondering "what if…." and worrying about all sorts of things. That's part of being human. But sometimes things become more complicated, and it's important to know when what's going on is a bit more serious – whether it's happening to you, a family member or a friend.

A mental illness is a condition that affects a person's thinking, feeling or mood and may affect their ability to get on with others or just get through the day – the symptoms can be so bad that they cause lots of stress and affect their ability to function. Examples of mental illnesses are depression, anxiety disorders, schizophrenia, eating disorders and addictive behaviours. A mental illness can make you miserable and can cause problems in your daily life at school or work or in relationships. In most cases, symptoms can be managed with a combination of medications and talking to someone professionally qualified to help.

If a friend or family member is diagnosed with a mental illness it's important that you don't take on the responsibility of trying to fix them, and make sure you have someone to talk to who can help you too.

> "THE BEST THING YOU CAN DO IS SPEND TIME WITH YOUR FRIEND AND HAVE FUN WITH HER, WITHOUT EXPECTING HER TO BE THE 'OLD' HER."

Dear Katie,

I'm worried about my friend who has told me she was recently diagnosed with depression. She hasn't told any of my other friends about this, so if they ask me if I know what is wrong with her I have to lie, which is hard. I keep trying to talk to my friend but she changes the subject, and whenever she does tell me things, I don't know how to reply to her. Recently I've seen cuts on her arms and I know she's self-harming. I'm not sure if her family or counsellor know about this and I get really scared and upset, worrying that she might hurt herself really badly. I want to talk to her about her mental health, but I'm not sure how to bring it up in a conversation, as I'm worried that I will just upset her.

From Me

Hey You,

Thanks so much for writing to me. It's wonderful to see you caring for your friend and wanting to help her.

I'm so sad that she's going through such a tough time. I'm so happy to see that she has a strong group of friends who care about her and want to talk to her about how she's feeling. I have suffered from depression and have friends who have too. This won't be the first time in your life that you encounter this dreaded illness, I'm sure. You may find you or other friends or family end up suffering from it yourself at some point. Sometimes we don't realise that people close to us are depressed, because it isn't something that everyone feels they can talk about. We often mistake symptoms of depression as people being moody, quiet, mean or boring. We don't know what is going on in someone's life, and in someone's mind. Depression and other mental health problems are more common than we think – approximately 1 in 4 people will experience a mental health problem each year, and 1 in 10 children (people aged 0–18) have a diagnosed mental health disorder – that's roughly 3 in every classroom. But more people than this struggle with their emotions, they just haven't been diagnosed. Many people aren't receiving any help or aren't aware they have an illness – some people believe it's just their personality or the way life is supposed to be.

Depression does not discriminate. I had depression when I was working as a TV presenter with a loving family, boyfriend, friends – everything I wanted, with the world at my feet. I knew that my life was perfect, but I was still incredibly insecure and full of anxiety and self-hatred. I felt worthless. We don't always know why people are depressed – they might not even know where it came from themselves. Anyone can be depressed, and plenty of celebrities who seemingly 'have it all' have suffered and spoken about it openly, such as Zoella, Frankie Bridge and Lady Gaga. Depression is an illness and, like a physical illness, anyone can get it at any time.

When I was depressed, there are two things I wanted people to do.

1. Leave me alone. I used to hide in the toilets at work just to have a few extra minutes of not having to fake a smile or talk to anyone. I used to find it painful to say hello to friends, or answer their 'How are you?' questions when they asked about me in passing. I felt frustrated when those who knew about my depression pushed me about it and asked if I felt better. I used to cry, not wanting to leave the house, unable to bear the thought of going out and socialising, already late to meet a friend I would have previously been excited to see. When my sister heard how I was feeling, she invited me for dinner to chat. Usually, I'd snatch her hand off to spend time with

her – she's wonderful and I love her – but I remember saying no. I didn't care about letting people down. I felt drained and sometimes had physical symptoms – depression can sometimes manifest itself physically, with headaches, nausea, feeling tired and achy. I just wanted to sleep, even though I'd have terrible nightmares when I did.

Try not to put demands on your friend. Don't expect her to be animated and chatty and fun any more than you would expect a friend with a headache or the flu to be the same. Tell her that you just want to hang out with her – sit and watch telly, read magazines, play on your phones together or watch a film. Tell her you don't care if she doesn't want to talk to you that whole time, but if she does you are there to listen. Tell her you just want her company. She needs yours too, she just doesn't have enough willpower left to care about keeping up her friendships. She's sick and tired.

At the same time, don't let her get into her own little hole which she might never come out of. She still needs your help. Just like I needed my sister's help when she pushed me that evening and asked me again to go for dinner with her. That night was the first time I properly spoke to someone about my depression and the night I started to get better. (Plus we had cake, and cake is good.) This brings me to the second thing I wanted people to do when I was depressed . . .

2. Help me. I didn't have the energy or the will to ask for help. I didn't care about myself any more, but I did need help. I needed someone to tell me that it was all going to be fine, and that with the right help I would be happy again. I wouldn't have believed them, but perhaps I would have seen my doctor sooner. When I did go and see my GP, they helped me straight away and – guess what? – I'm now happier than I've ever been. Your friend will be too, I'm sure.

It's hard to advise people without upsetting them – it's hard to know what the right 'level' of encouragement is. But if your friend does speak to you and gives you a few words about how she's feeling, use the opportunity to point her towards some professional advice. There are helplines at the back of this book.

You have done the right thing by not discussing this with your friends, as it isn't your news to tell. If your friend doesn't want the others in your group to know, then respect her wishes. You could tell your friends you don't know the details, but that you think your friend is feeling down at the moment. Being a friend to a person with depression can be very difficult, so if you feel like you want to talk about it, confide in a parent or another trusted adult, such as an older sibling or teacher. It's important you have somebody to talk to as well – you must look after your own mental health too.

This is my own personal perspective on what I would want a friend to do if I was feeling depressed, but everyone is different, so try asking your friend what she really wants from you. I would have appreciated it if someone had said that to me.

I asked our experts to give you some advice about depression, which you'll find below. She helps not only those with depression but those who care for people with depression every day, so she has some great tips to help you support your friend AND yourself.

You are a flipping wonderful person, by the way. Everyone should have a friend like you.

Love,
Katie xxx

DR RADHA SAYS

It is important to be able to recognise the symptoms of depression. They could include:
• Lack of interest in hobbies

- Lack of interest or enjoyment in socialising
- Lack of energy
- Oversleeping or not being able to sleep
- Overeating or not eating much
- Feelings of hopelessness and sadness
- Difficulty motivating themselves
- Not looking after themselves physically

Everyone goes through periods of feeling down, but if these symptoms persist for two weeks or more it may be a sign that there's something more serious going on.

TIPS TO HELP IF YOU THINK SOMEONE MAY BE DEPRESSED:
- Let them know you care and you are there to listen
- Do not judge them
- Ask open questions like 'I've noticed you're looking tired – are you feeling ok?' Open up the conversation in a quiet environment, so they feel they can chat
- Do not tell them 'You have nothing to feel sad about' or 'Snap out of it and you'll feel better soon'. Let them know you recognise how they feel and do not disregard their feelings
- Be patient
- Keep in touch with them regularly. Try to balance contacting them but also letting them have space
- Encourage them to talk to a professional, like a doctor

or a counsellor
- Encourage them to get out and be active. Exercise – even if it's just a walk outside – can help a lot
- Do not take on too much yourself – if you are worried that someone is really depressed, suicidal, or at risk of harming themselves, you must tell a trusted adult as soon as you can – this is too much for you to deal with on your own, and that person needs professional help

THERAPIST SALLY SAYS

Depression stems from a chemical imbalance in the brain and can make people feel sad, angry and withdrawn – sometimes for no apparent reason. Sometimes depression is a response to something that happens and sometimes it can just arrive uninvited. It's different from feeling sad because it lasts a long time and can cause you to have thoughts that make you feel very bad about yourself. It can stop you wanting to go out or do anything, and you can feel hopeless. The good news is that depression can be treated if you ask for help. Talking to someone you trust is a good start and your GP can help with a therapist or medication.

It's a very tough thing to be with someone who's

depressed, and depression can happen to anyone and can last a long time. As a friend or family member, you may go through a range of difficult emotions yourself – helplessness, confusion, anger, sadness – be aware that you also need someone to talk to, so find someone who can be there for you too. Make sure you take care of yourself – as they say on airlines, put on your own oxygen mask before helping others. You cannot fix someone with depression, so the most important thing is to make sure that they are getting professional help. Let them know that you are there for them even if they seem to reject you. Sometimes just listening can be amazingly helpful.

NOTES

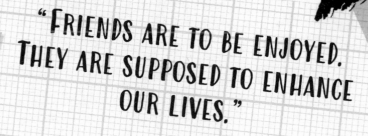

> "FRIENDS ARE TO BE ENJOYED. THEY ARE SUPPOSED TO ENHANCE OUR LIVES."

Dear Katie,

Me and my friend had a small argument yesterday and we are friends again now. But that's the problem: I don't want to be her friend. I just don't know what to do.

From Me

Dear Katie,

One of my friends wants to break up with me and I do not know what to do. Please could you help me? When you were in school, did one of your friends break up with you, and what did you do? If you were me, what would you do? Do I try to be friends with them again?

From Me

Hey Both of You

Friendships can be so hard! I wanted to answer your letters together because it's interesting to see the connection between the two of you. One of you wants to break up with a friend and the other has had that done to them. What a minefield! What you both have learned is that sometimes friends grow apart and no longer want to spend time with each other.

I believe that we should be kind to everyone, because you never know what somebody is going through, and your smile, conversation or acknowledgement could mean a lot to somebody. But I also believe that some people don't make us feel good. Some people make us feel unhappy.

And we don't have to give those people a starring role in the play of our lives.

This might sound punchy, but no one owes us their friendship. If one of our friends wants to break up with us, as hurtful as it may be, we need to remember that they are doing it for their own reasons. It isn't a reflection on you, but on their particular needs and issues at the time. It's easy to worry that your friend doesn't want to see you any more because you're not cool enough or fun enough, but even if those are the reasons, it's the issue of the friend and not you. If she wants a new group of friends, it might because she is insecure and wants to try to gain popularity. Whatever her reasons may be, which you might find out in time, we can't change the actions of others. We must focus on what we CAN change. We can decide to join clubs to make new friends, we can take up new hobbies to occupy our time, we can be kind to people we know. We can choose to accept that our friend has dropped us and pick ourselves up and carry on, start making new friends and doing the things we enjoy.

At the same time, it's OK to feel hurt by the situation. Losing someone you once had a friendship with is hard, and it's perfectly acceptable to feel bad about it and allow yourself some time to grieve. Talking about problems like this can help us feel better and figure out our real feelings about the situation, so try talking to another friend or family member about it.

If you have a friendship which is making you unhappy, it can be hard to drop that person. You might think you'll be able to work things out, that their annoying habits are just a phase, or that you have suffocated each other by spending too much time together. Sometimes this is the case. Even my closest friends annoy me sometimes. The best of mates insult each other when they've simply had enough, only for them to be madly back in friend-love a week later. Often our friends annoy us because we care about them – they might be acting differently all of a sudden because of something going on in their own life. Sometimes we get frustrated because in our opinion our friends are making the wrong decisions. Often we become jealous of our friends, because we are going through an insecure phase, or they can become jealous of us for the same reason and say hurtful things as a result. Sometimes we think that there's something 'better' out there, that the next person will be the perfect friend, so we keep going round and round, trying out new people. Even though the perfect friend or perfect person doesn't exist! Have a think about whether one of these scenarios sounds like your situation – if so, you might just need a little breathing space or a friendly chat about it. Sometimes friendships just shift, too. A friendship doesn't have to be all or nothing – maybe only hanging sometimes and not every day will sort the problem.

Friendships come in all different shapes and sizes, and change over time too.

Sometimes friends just grow apart. When we are young, we tend to make our friends due to geography – they live on our street, they are in our class, our parents are friends. As time goes on and you start to build more interests, and growing up makes you develop into different people, you may start to realise that you don't enjoy a particular friendship anymore. Perhaps you make more friends or start secondary school and your group expands. Maybe you drift apart, though that doesn't necessarily mean cutting old friends out of your life.

Friends are to be enjoyed. They are supposed to enhance our lives. I have had to distance myself from friends who have picked on my faults in front of a group, because they were damaging my self-esteem. I have had to distance myself from friends because we had become two such different people that I was not able to be myself with them.

I encourage you to be kind to everyone, but remember that your time is valuable. If the time you spend with someone isn't making you feel good, either gradually make that time less and less or chat to them and let them know you're going to be spending a bit more time with other friends. Decide what's best, depending on the situation and the feelings of those involved. It will all work out OK, as long as you both have friends to turn to. You don't need to be best friends with someone and take them with you everywhere for as long as you live, if you don't want to. Your friendships shape your life and general happiness more than you realise – we learn from friends and adapt our behaviour depending on theirs – so choose wisely and focus on yourself, and don't feel bad about doing so.

Be kind, for everyone you know is fighting a battle.

Love,
Katie xxx

THERAPIST SALLY SAYS

Jealousy can get confused with envy, but whereas envy is usually about wanting something someone else has, jealousy is more about fear of being replaced or losing something that is precious to us. Jealousy usually occurs because we don't believe in ourselves enough. Jealousy ususally results in an unpleasant stew of emotions including feeling angry, frightened of losing someone or just not feeling good enough. It often comes along and niggles away at trust both in us and in our friends, siblings or partners. Sometimes jealousy can make you want to be more controlling and the critic inside your head might really go into overdrive. Work on building your confidence and self-esteem – and ask other friends and family members to support you.

Envy usually stems from seeing something which someone else has, wanting it for yourself, but feeling like you can't have it. Envy can lead to all sorts of uncomfortable feelings about yourself and the person who you envy. You might feel shame, inferiority, anger, sick to your stomach, or a sense of it's just not fair. Envy often hides a lack of confidence or feelings of shame, because somewhere you don't feel deserving. One of the secrets is to focus less on other people. Instead of imagining how great their life is, make a point of focusing on what's good in yours. Social media only fuels the flames of envy. So stay away from that Instagram feed!

The positive flip side of envy can be inspiration, but make sure you're not chasing something that someone else has just because they have it. Make time to think about what would make you really happy and see the things in yourself that are good and unique. Focus on what makes you who you are and follow your own dreams: the most important thing is to be true to yourself.

NOTES

Dear Katie,

Someone from my old school keeps being horrible to me, and her mum keeps covering for her. It's making my friends think that I'm the one being nasty, but I'm not. It's really making me upset. What should I do?

From Me

Hey You,

Oh dear, mums love their children so much that
sometimes they can't comprehend that their child might
be the one being mean. Mums are people too and
sometimes they're mean. They are also sometimes wrong.
That's really frustrating for you. The only thing worse than
someone being mean to you is other people not believing
you and thinking YOU are the mean one! The injustice of
it all is maddening.

Can you identify why you and this person aren't getting
along? Is it something one of you did? Is she being mean
because she is going through something difficult in her
life and projecting that on to you? Could you have a chat
with her one-on-one and ask her how she is or if you have
done something to upset her? This might not work, and the
person might just be being mean, but it's worth a try.

If that doesn't work, you need to find a way of dealing
with the situation as it stands. As human beings we love
to gossip, and the more you discuss these incidents with
your friends the more they will chat about it. Perhaps
they will come up with theories about what is going on
– including the theory that you are the mean one, when
that simply isn't true. We love to speculate.

And that's what you need to avoid. The best way to

diffuse this situation is to stop adding fuel to the fire –
the fuel being the dialogue between you, this mean girl,
and your friends. I believe that if you stop talking about
something you want people to forget all about, they
eventually will.

In short, if talking to this person doesn't work, ignore
her. Be civil with her and avoid her as much as possible.
You say she's from an old school – how are you still in
contact? If it's through social media, ignore her messages
or block her. Brush off her mean comments. Don't rise to
it. Don't give her anything to use and she will get bored.

Meanwhile, don't discuss it with your friends. Don't say
mean things about the girl, because even if you haven't
'started it', talking about her will make you mean too.
Your friends will forget about their theory that you are the
nasty one soon enough if you are being kind to everyone.

Confide in someone you can trust, who won't judge
you or gossip about you – someone who will just listen.
A parent or guardian or sibling or other older family
member. This way you'll have someone to talk to safely.
Someone you can trust, outside of the group involved,
who won't spread rumours about you, who will support
you. My parents were great for this when I was going
through some tough times with friends at school, along
with my cousin and a friend who lived far away. These

people were all separate from the situation and I could vent to them without worrying I was stirring the pot further! Find the people who you can talk to, hold your head up high and be the person you want to be.

Love,
Katie xxx

THERAPIST SALLY SAYS

Sometimes the feelings and thoughts we have about ourselves are a bit too much for us and we don't like them, so – without realising it – we convince ourselves that they belong to other people. This is called projection. Then we blame them or perhaps think they're better than us. Projecting difficult feelings on to people is something bullies do to others – because they don't like themselves very much.

Carl Jung thought that we hid the really good things as well as the bad in what he called the 'shadow'. He thought that the shadow was where we could find our true gifts. So remember, sometimes we might even convince ourselves that the good things in us belong to other people too, because we can't accept how incredible we are!

> ## "I WENT THROUGH A PHASE OF FEELING SO SCARED AT SCHOOL I USED TO COUNT DOWN THE HOURS TO HOME TIME."

Dear Katie,

A couple of weeks ago, I was at the park with my friends and these girls were having a go at us. Then I saw one of them at the shop and she came up to me and said I'd been calling her horrible names on social media, when I hadn't. She said she wanted a fight with me and was going to drag me out of the shop. I refused to fight her and went and called my mum. The girl said if she ever sees me again she'll beat me up. I play out in my local area a lot and she is often there – I'm really scared that she will hurt me.

From Me

Hey You,

I'm sorry to hear that this has happened to you. I hate situations like this.

Once when I was a teenager, I was walking to my friend's house when I saw a boy I knew talking to two girls from my school. I hadn't ever spoken to the girls but I knew who they were – I'd seen them around and I found them a bit scary. When they walked away the boy approached me and said, "Those girls were looking for you. They said they were going to beat you up, but I told them to go away." I was shocked. I didn't even know the girls' names – why did they want to beat me up? I always kept myself to myself. I didn't have any enemies, not that I was aware of. The boy didn't know why either. I'm sure they didn't know.

Some people just want to fight, or feel like they need to fight. Or rather, some people just want to SAY they want to fight. That's because of a problem they have, not you. After that day, I occasionally ran into those girls at school and in my local area, but they didn't once lay a finger on me – didn't even say a word. They might have said they wanted to beat me up to appear tough and to impress the boy or their mates. They might have been showing off in front of each other. For whatever reason, some people think that behaving in a mean and aggressive manner makes them respected and admired. I don't respect or admire people who fight or hurt others, but some people do. Strange, right? For some, keeping people fearful is what they thrive on. It makes them feel in control, and that they can't be harmed mentally or physically because they are busy doing the harming.

The girl who threatened you needs help with her issues. When you're a teenager, hormones are all over the place and minds and bodies are changing, and this can cause problems. This girl may have learned this behaviour from her parents or other family members and knows no other way to act. She probably lied about you saying things on social media as an excuse to have someone to pick on. I hope that her words are just that – words – empty threats to try to scare you and to appear big in front of her mates. I hope she doesn't ever come near you again.

That said, it's still scary to be threatened. I was scared when I heard those two girls wanted to beat me up. I didn't know how to fight. I still don't! I didn't want to be beaten up, and neither do you. I used to be terrified that I would see them on the way to school, and want to stay at home most days so I could avoid them. I went through a phase of feeling so scared at school I would count down the hours to home time. After each lesson I would think 'I've survived another hour'. I'd get home to my safe haven and watch TV and feel relaxed and relieved. Eventually I realised that they weren't going to bother with me – soon they didn't care any more, if they even did in the first place.

Speak to your mum again about her and explain that you're hoping she will forget all about the confrontation, but until then ask if you can play somewhere else in your local area. Perhaps your mum will let you invite your friends to your house instead. It isn't fair that you should suffer or have to stop doing the things you like because of this, but I want you to be safe first and foremost, so if you can have fun somewhere else where this girl won't be, then try that. The less she sees you, the sooner she will forget about making you her victim, and soon some other poor person will be. At the same time, make your social media private, so that she can't see it and accuse you of writing anything about her.

If your mum knows her parents, she could speak to them, or her school if you know which school she goes to. She needs help to stop harming people in this way. I'm sure this can be done discreetly so it doesn't cause you any trouble – I'm certain you're not the only person she has picked on, so it doesn't need to be obvious that the complaints have come from you.

You did the right thing when she first tried to pick a fight, so I know you will do the right thing again.

Love,
Katie xxx

NOTES

"YOU'RE NOT IN CHARGE OF WHAT OTHER PEOPLE DO, BUT YOU ARE IN CONTROL OF YOUR OWN ACTIONS."

Dear Katie,

My absolute best friend went out with a boy, and then she dumped him. I am now going out with him and she isn't talking to me. Help – I can't live without either of them and I don't know what to do. Please reply.

From Me

Hey You,

Uh-oh, you've learned an age-old lesson here – friends don't always stay friends when they share boyfriends or girlfriends. We are jealous beings and protective of those we choose to date, sometimes even when we're not dating them any more. Your friend might not want to go out with this boy now, and she may have been the one to dump him, but having someone so close to her going out with him – i.e. you, her best friend – is probably making her feel uncomfortable or betrayed. Or perhaps she feels you have broken an unwritten rule. Everyone has their own different 'rules' when it comes to this kind of thing. I asked a few people your age about what they would do in this situation and how they would feel. Some people thought your friend was right to be annoyed at you and others thought that you should be cross with your friend, as if she didn't want to go out with the boy she should want you to be happy. I'm not here to tell you what the right or wrong answer is, because that can only be decided by you, but this demonstrated how people can feel very differently about what is right and wrong in our relationships.

What I am here to tell you is that you CAN live without both of these people – you can live without anyone. You are brilliant and powerful and capable on your own. However, it sounds as though you don't WANT to have to live without them. You obviously value both of them. This doesn't need to be the end.

If you continue going out with the boy, you might not be able to have your best friend. She has already made it clear that she feels you have crossed a line, by stopping speaking to you. She might change her mind, but she might not. You might not be able to change it for her. We can't control others. Whether or not you agree with someone's decision to stop being your friend, people have their own reasons – their own rules – and we have to respect these. However, you can talk to her and see if there's anything you can do. Maybe she wants an apology. Maybe she doesn't want to hang out with you while your boyfriend is around. Maybe she needs some time.

If you stop going out with the boy, and explain to your best friend that you've done that in order to rebuild your friendship with her, as you miss her and have realised your actions hurt her, you might get her back. You might be able to keep the boy's friendship too. But it might be too late with your friend, and the boy might not be interested in being just friends with you.

You might lose both of them as friends, or you might keep them in your circle but with changed relationships. If you get your best friend back, it might take a while for things to return to how they were. But remember what I said earlier about how you can survive without anyone, so most importantly, look after yourself. There are many positive elements to your life and many people who you can have a friendship with.

You're not in charge of what other people do, but you are in control of your own actions. You can do what you think is right, and be content with that decision, knowing that you've done the right thing. Put your own happiness first, while trying not to hurt anyone in the process.

Write down the different options, the pros and cons, and read them back to yourself until the penny drops. You know what to do.

Love,
Katie xxx

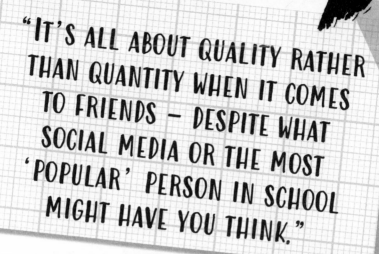

"IT'S ALL ABOUT QUALITY RATHER THAN QUANTITY WHEN IT COMES TO FRIENDS — DESPITE WHAT SOCIAL MEDIA OR THE MOST 'POPULAR' PERSON IN SCHOOL MIGHT HAVE YOU THINK."

Dear Katie,

I am really shy and I struggle to talk to new people. It never really bothered me until about a month ago when I started at secondary school. I have only made a couple of friends in this whole term and I am constantly scared of losing them. Throughout the morning I feel scared and worried that I will end up being alone at break and lunch, despite the fact that it has only happened once since I started. Deep down I know that I will be OK, I just don't know how to make my mind see it too.

Also, I really enjoy sports and there are a number of sports clubs running at lunchtimes at my new school, but I am terrified to go to them alone. I keep skipping sessions because I don't know anybody else who is going. I know that I should just take a deep breath and go for it, but I just can't bring myself to do it.

One last thing – there is a gymnastics club outside of school that I have been going to for nearly three years, yet I don't have any friends there. Everybody talks and messes around with each other, while I am on my own talking to nobody. This only started to bother me recently and I feel like it is too late to make friends there now. Everybody is either a lot older than me or a lot younger and I feel like the odd one out. Thank you for reading, and I really hope you can help!

From Me

Hey You,

Being shy does not mean you are boring, or unworthy of friends. Just because you perhaps lack confidence does not mean you should have to feel lonely. Being the quiet one isn't a bad thing! Sometimes the loud ones can come across as obnoxious and annoying – shyer people are more mysterious, interesting and approachable, and less intimidating to others.

Don't ever feel like you're not a wonderful person, or inferior to everybody else because you are shy. You are perfect as you are and you can be whoever you want to be. What's important is that you're comfortable with yourself. If worrying less about losing your current friends and making some new friends at your club is going to make you feel better, then let's do it!

It's all about quality rather than quantity when it comes to friends – despite what social media or the most 'popular' person in school might have you think. It's great that you've made a couple of friends at secondary school – it can be really difficult to do that. It sounds as though your self-confidence might be low, as you're worried that you're going to lose your friends or be left alone – despite, as you said, that being very unlikely indeed. Our brain can be naughty like that – it makes us worry about things we don't need to.

Other people bring us lots of happiness – and unhappiness from time to time too. We are social beings who interact with others by nature, but we do spend time worrying about how we would cope if we lost a loved one, split up with a boyfriend or girlfriend, fell out with a friend . . . Often we are worrying about these things for no reason, as they might never happen, or at least not for a very long time. Even if they do happen, they might be out of our control, and worrying won't fix anything. And if we're worrying about something which may or may not happen in the future, we are missing what is happening in the present. I do it – I'll be sitting with my family/boyfriend/friends, and worrying about what life would be like if I didn't have them around or if they stopped spending time with me. While it's important to be aware of your priorities – what you really care about and who you really care about – by worrying when we are with those people, we are missing out on enjoying those moments! If we are making the most of our time with them, being the best friend we can be, and letting them help us grow and feel happy, we'd get much more out of our relationships. The irony is that we can push people away, or not enjoy our time with them, because we are too busy worrying about losing them.

First, try something for me – try being your own best friend. I used to worry so much about losing my friends when I was younger, and always tried to have as many friends as possible. But actually, most were acquaintances, not friends – people to pass time with, part of a bigger group in which only a couple of people were my real friends, whose company I loved and enjoyed. Nowadays, rather than trying to amass as many people as possible to call friends, I enjoy my own company a lot. I've figured out who I am – what I like and dislike, what my hobbies and passions, my goals and dreams and fears are. I'm kind to myself and don't make myself do anything I don't want to do. I allow myself time for self-care – like watching my favourite TV show or having a nap. I know that no matter who comes or goes in my life, as long as I'm alive I have myself and I have those things that I enjoy. So be your best friend, figure out who you are and what you like, and you will worry less about having to rely on others for happiness.

Second, enjoy your time with your friends at school and be a good friend to them. Ask them questions about their lives and ask them for help when you need it – these are sure-fire ways of encouraging people to like you. I'm sure they already do. I'm sure they worry about losing you as much as you worry about losing them. But it's common to fear this. I used to come away from social situations and worry about how I'd come across – was I interesting enough? Did I say something which might have offended someone? Did I pay a certain person enough attention? What if they don't want to see me any more? What if they don't value me as a proper friend? I soon realised as I got older that everyone has these anxieties, and as long as I was being myself and treating people how I would want to be treated, then I shouldn't worry, because we can't control other people. We can only be the person we want to be, be content with that and enjoy ourselves. That's your power. No one can take YOU away from you. You are your best friend, who can be loyal to the end.

Third, accept that you are shy. It is one of your brilliant character traits which make you unique. Admit that you are shy. Tell new people you meet that you're shy – they will sympathise with you, and probably like you more for it. They might be shy themselves! Lots of people are shy, but simply fake their confidence – I know I do. I used to be scared about meeting new people, but I would pretend I wasn't, and talk to them confidently. Over time, this fake confidence became a real confidence, and now the idea of meeting new people excites me.

My job helped me with my confidence. I was a nervous wreck when I started presenting on TV – I had to fake my confidence completely. But no one notices the difference between fake confidence and real confidence, and if you can move from one to the other, all of a sudden your life will be much easier.

You could use your hobbies to make a start with this. I understand how nerve-wracking it is to go to an afterschool club on your own. I too would have been terrified. I'd worry that my peers would judge me. I'd be scared about sitting alone. I'd think everyone would be watching every move I made. But in reality, none of this would happen. Nowadays I'll sit in a restaurant and eat alone, but once upon a time I wouldn't have dreamed of doing such a thing. Now I just own it. I'm eating on my own and I don't care who knows! Table for one please!

This is what you could do at those sports sessions you want to go to. Turn up, head held high, full of (perhaps fake) confidence. If you're the only one there who went alone, guess what that makes you? The most confident person there. Nobody else had the guts to do that. They are there with friends they perhaps BEGGED to join them because – guess what? – they felt exactly the same as you.

Sports are a great way to socialise when you're shy – you're all there because you're interested in that activity, so you already have something in common, plus you have something to do! Once everyone starts the session, it won't matter who came with friends or not, what matters is the sport! Every man/woman for him/herself, and no time for chatting! One tip that I've always found useful is to turn up early and get talking to one person.

This is a technique I use when I go into schools to do shows for people like you. I find that experience scary – large groups of schoolchildren can be intimidating, as you'll know! Sometimes I get chatting to one or two people at the front, and then when I go up on stage, I already feel like a couple of kids in the room have got my back. We've already formed a bond. I've spoken to some of them and realised they're not going to bite. See – I'm still using these techniques. I present in front of audiences and on live television every day, but I still get nervous talking to new people – we all do. You're not alone. You don't have to imagine the people are all in their undies (a classic confidence-building technique), but you could imagine they're feeling just as shy as you – because they most likely are.

One last thing – when I was in my second year of secondary school, I was quite popular and got a bit cocky. One of my friends made a joke about me, and I decided to ignore her and the others who had laughed for a few days. I was being too big for my boots – I did it to assert my authority – and it backfired. All of the group fell out with me. Only two friends stuck by me – one of them is still my best friend today. School was a nightmare for me for the next few months – the people who were once my friends bullied me, and I became extremely shy and nervous and a completely different person to my former self. I wanted to skip school all the time. I couldn't bear walking into my own classroom. I felt like the world was against me. I survived though – we all ended up being friends again, and my confidence came back eventually, but it taught me a very important lesson. Never think I'm better than other people or get too cocky, as my situation can soon change. It also taught me that we ARE our own best friends, and we will survive, even if the whole world turns against us. I've got to know myself a lot more in moments when I've felt alone, and this helped me to become a more resilient person, and shaped who I am today.

The new friends you're about to meet don't realise how lucky they are – they're soon to have a brilliant new friend in the form of you.

Here's to the shy kids!

Love,
Katie xxx

THERAPIST SALLY SAYS

Does the idea of going to a party fill you with excitement, and staying in on a Saturday night fill you with dread? If so, you're what Carl Jung described as an extravert personality. If it's the other way around and you can think of nothing worse than being surrounded by lots of people talking and having fun – you probably have an introvert personality. Being an introvert often gets mistaken for being shy, but really it's all about what gives you energy. As an introvert you need 'me' time to recharge, whereas an extravert will prefer to go out and be with people.

Shyness can sometimes be caused by bad experiences and imagined situations that we want to avoid because we feel bad about ourselves or worried about what might happen. It can be linked to low self-esteem and fear of being embarrassed. We all feel shy from time to time – naturally cautious about new and unknown things. But if you're avoiding social situations all the time and suffering from anxiety about talking to other people, it might be worth seeing a CBT therapist, who can help you with some very practical steps to overcome your fears.

> # "YOU ARE ANYONE YOU WANT TO BE — NOBODY CAN DEFINE YOUR IDENTITY WITHOUT YOUR PERMISSION."

Dear Katie,

I was outed as bisexual about a year ago. Two of my friends were outed at the same time. Even though a year has gone by, people still don't treat me as a person. I'm known as the weird gay girl, not as that girl who is a fan of Harry Potter or that girl who likes music. Not even as my name. I can't go in the girls' changing rooms without people thinking I'm looking at them. I also get comments all the time about me wanting to go out with my best friend. I'm finding it hard to deal with all the stress, especially with exams coming up. Please help.

From Me

Hey You,

I'm so sorry to hear you have been treated this way. This is unacceptable behaviour towards you and we must do what we can to make it better.

I went to an all-girls secondary school, and the comments you refer to remind me of that. You had to practically keep your eyes closed in the changing rooms at school, for fear you'd accidentally glance at someone, and a bully accuse you of being a lesbian trying to look at her boobies.

Unfortunately, some teenagers often behave in this way. Some adults do too. I hate to tell you this, but some adults act like they're still at school. We do not live in a perfect world, and while YOU know and I know that there is nothing wrong with being bisexual, SOME people do not have the same opinion. Some people are WRONG.

We usually refer to people like this as 'ignorant', which means they lack understanding. In your case, they lack an understanding of bisexuality. Or rather, they haven't tried to understand. Instead of accepting you are different to them, but also equal, they have decided that the difference is an issue. This might be because they have picked up prejudiced opinions from others – perhaps views on sexuality have been passed on to them by their family or friends. It may be because they are insecure about themselves. By deflecting this on to you, and acting like YOU are the weird one, they can feel less weird themselves and hope that nobody notices something about THEM that THEY feel insecure about.

You will come across people like this from time to time, but I would bet my special edition Harry Potter book that things will get easier than they are right now. Secondary school is a strange place, where it feels like everything is how it will always be. I remember moving from secondary school to college, and some of the bullies from school claimed they were going to be the most popular girls there. But once we had all separated from our comfort groups and joined colleges filled with people from different schools who we'd never met before, they lost their power. In college, there were people who were gay, straight, bisexual, transgender – people from all different walks of life. And do you know what else? NONE of these people were either bullies or victims. It will get better.

I can't promise that your experience of college will be as positive as mine – like you, I can't be sure of anything that's going to happen to you – but you CAN remember that every time you feel someone is treating you differently or unfairly because of your sexuality, the problem is with THEM, not you. It is they who need to be cured – of their ignorance. They are the ones missing out on your friendship – missing out on having friendships with people different to them. It will make their lives significantly less fulfilling in the long run. Take it from someone who has grown up with gay friends and straight friends and bisexual friends and seen all this happen. You're going to come out of this stronger.

They are the weird ones, and do you know who you are? YOU are the girl who is a fan of Harry Potter. YOU are the girl who likes music. YOU are anyone you want to be – nobody can define your identity without your permission.

Treat yourself with respect first and foremost, even when others don't.

Love,
Katie xxx

> # "TRY NOT TO WORRY ABOUT WHAT OTHER PEOPLE ARE DOING. ALL THAT MATTERS IS THAT YOU ARE DOING WHATEVER YOU WANT TO DO."

Dear Katie,

Until recently I haven't ever had a crush on anyone at all. I thought it was completely normal until I started talking to my classmates about it and realised it was not. Then a few weeks ago I started to feel what I think is a crush on a girl who goes to the same out-of-school club as me. But because this hasn't happened before I don't know for sure.

I'm happy when I'm around her and she's always really kind, but I don't understand what I'm feeling. My family and friends are completely accepting and coming out isn't a worry for me.

My friendship group is similar to how it was in primary school, except I feel as if I am being replaced by other people. My friends never seem to want me to do things with them and I'm always their last choice if they want to talk or hang out with anyone. It's like they're avoiding me and just think of me as an irritant. Sometimes it's like there's a hierarchy within the group, and me and a few others are at the bottom.

Please help!

From Me

Hey You,

First of all, it's fine if you haven't had a crush yet. Just because your group of friends have, doesn't make you abnormal for not feeling the same as them. Hey, maybe you are just pickier than they are and you haven't met anyone you like in that way yet! We all develop at different stages. Don't feel like you need to rush to develop a crush because your friends are – crushes are complicated and they don't always involve feeling good, so just enjoy your life and try not to worry about what other people claim to be going through. You're not missing out. (And remember that people tell white lies when chatting to their mates about this kind of thing!) You say you are unsure about whether or not you have a crush on a friend of yours who is a girl, like you. I'm really pleased that your family are supportive, so coming out wouldn't be a problem for you – that's brilliant. You may have a crush on this girl, it may develop, and you may reach the point where you decide to come out to your family and friends as a girl who is interested in girls, or a girl who is interested in both boys and girls.

On the other hand, crushes on same-sex friends, even if you're not gay, are common too. I remember being your age and beginning to fancy people. I had crush-like feelings for a girl I knew. Like you do with your friend, I felt happy when I was around her. I thought she was so cool. I respected her and admired her. I wasn't sure if I wanted to BE her or be her girlfriend. The feeling wore off, and since then I haven't had any more crushes on girls, only stinky boys. It turned out I was straight after all, but my feelings had been so strong towards this friend of mine that I had wondered back then if it might be something more than admiration.

This might be what's happening to you, or it might not – it's impossible for me, or anyone else, to tell you what your sexuality is. For now, try not to worry about what other people are doing, or say they are doing – whether they are straight or gay or bisexual or having crushes or not or having relationships or not. All that matters is that you are doing whatever you want to do. That's all you have to do. Whatever you WANT to do. Feeling happy around someone can only ever be a good thing, so enjoy that relationship.

When I think back to my girl crush, the strong feelings I felt towards her were because she was a new addition to my life, and had a personality I admired and had long been looking for in a friend. I'd experienced some problems at school – falling out with people in my friendship group, being bullied – and while all that had blown over, a part of me probably still felt insecure in my current group of friends. This new person hadn't been a part of all the previous dramas I'd had with friends. She thought I was cool and liked me and seemed to be on the same wavelength as me, and what I felt for her was strong, even though I now know that it was a passing feeling and that I'm not gay. This could be what is happening for you right now – things are a bit 'up in the air' in your school friendship group and so developing a friendship with someone separate from that is very attractive to you.

Enjoy this new friendship, because it sounds happy and positive – just what you need at a time when your school group isn't making you feel that way. It's great to have an escape from that hierarchical world and have an 'outside of school' friend. Your feelings for her will most likely become clearer and you may realise that the girl crush was a passing phase and little more than admiration. Or your feelings might continue and grow stronger. You might decide you want to talk to somebody about your sexuality. There are helplines at the back of this book for that situation. Don't forget that you're never alone in how you're feeling – someone else somewhere will be feeling that way too. I'm sure some of your friends are feeling equally confused about their crushes right now.

I'm excited for you – you have a whole life of friendships and crushes ahead of you. It's going to be confusing and difficult at times, but it's going to be wonderful too.

Love,
Katie xxx

THERAPIST SALLY SAYS

Love and sexual attraction are complex, and who we are attracted to can change over time. We might be attracted to all sorts of people throughout our lives:

male, female, non-binary, cis or transgender. Sexuality is a spectrum, and while some people would clearly describe themselves as hetero or homo sexual, lots of us are somewhere in between.

Sexual attraction can be confusing and overwhelming and we can feel under pressure to know who or what we like: boys or girls. Most people have felt some kind of attraction for someone of the same sex and for many it's something they move on from, for others this becomes the norm. It's not about being attracted to boys or girls, but about being attracted to a person, and whether that person is male or female can be of secondary importance. There can be lots of pressure to adopt an identity and to 'come out' but there's no right way or right time.

For many, it's just feeling free to talk about whoever they like or love. Maybe being open and public about how you feel feels right, maybe it doesn't. The most important thing is to be true to yourself, follow your instinct and know that it's fine to like boys or girls or boys and girls. And if a friend or family member or partner shifts, be compassionate and accepting — especially when other people might not be as understanding.

Dear Katie,

I'm thirteen and I've always been a very trendy person and because of that I wanted social media. I have Instagram without my parents knowing and some boys from my school who I had blocked got hold of my profile pic. It was a really cute one of me and my mum, and the boys started saying things about it in a group chat. I had no idea until the Internet Safety Teacher from my school took me out of a lesson and told me what had happened. I was shocked to the core. He said he would talk to my parents and I got really stressed. At home time my mum came to pick me up and she had a stern look on her face. I asked her what was wrong and she just lied to me and said she had a headache. When we got home she started interrogating me – both my mum and dad gave me a lecture and said that I could never have Instagram again. I still have it but I hide it on my phone, although I have been caught out a couple of times. I enjoy making videos and asked my parents if I could have a YouTube channel but they said no. I think it's because of the bullying prior to this. Please help me, Katie.

From Me

Hey You,

I feel your pain because, as you said, you're someone who likes to keep up with the trends, and social media – particularly Instagram and YouTube – is very popular and a huge part of many people's lives at the moment. (Although it certainly isn't the 'be all and end all'!)

It's great that you want to make videos, and I encourage you to do that whether or not your parents allow you to have a YouTube account. I used to write books and make magazines for my neighbour, and sometimes I'd make radio shows literally just for myself. It didn't matter that nobody saw this stuff – it was great practice for me, I enjoyed it, plus it kept me busy and gave me important skills and experience (which were beneficial to me as a student and later for my job!). If making videos is what you enjoy, making videos is what you shall do. You don't have to share them on a public YouTube account.

I'm sorry to hear that those boys spoilt things for you. Sadly, it's easy for people to get hold of profile pictures, even if you've blocked them. They are publicly available on most social networking sites, even if your profile is private. In fact, if you put in just about anyone's name to a search engine you will be able to find at least one or two pictures of them – even if they have tried their hardest to make their settings private. Nothing on the internet is truly private, and we have to remember that when we upload stuff. Sometimes the stuff you thought you had hidden crops up – scary!

You are probably right to think that your parents don't want you to have Instagram and YouTube because of this incident. Their ban on social media is to protect you. (When I was your age it was fashionable to have your belly button pierced like Britney Spears and my mum said I wasn't allowed. I said I would get it done AS SOON as I was old enough to not need her consent. By then, I was pretty over the idea and belly button piercings had gone out of fashion!)

I hate to say this, but your folks do have a point. Social media, as brilliant as it can be for sharing videos of cats/morphing your own face into a strawberry/hashtagging #squadgoals under a picture of you and your friends, has dangers too. There are bad people in the world and unfortunately the internet makes it a lot easier for people to be bad. Not just strangers, but people you know, who might be cyberbullying to make themselves feel a bit better – these are the stinkers you came across. Your parents didn't have Instagram and YouTube when they were your age and so they're worried about someone taking advantage of you.

That's not to say they won't come round to the idea, especially as you get older. Most social networking sites have a minimum age of fourteen years, so when you are fourteen they might reconsider. Perhaps, rather than sneakily downloading the app and then getting found out and told off every now and again, you could try a new approach and obey their rules. Prove that you have had a break from social media, and explain to them that there are good things about Instagram and YouTube, and ways you can minimise any trouble while using it.

For example, you can have a private Instagram account and YouTube account so that only people who you approve can see your stuff. You could tell your mum and dad that they are allowed to control this – so that they can check who is following you and what you're posting. This way, if something is worrying them, you can have a discussion about it and come to an agreement. Show them how it works – ask them to be involved. Admit you've been downloading it in secret but now you want to be honest about it, as you'd rather they were part of the experience so that they can help you to stay safe.

Whatever happens – whether they let you use Instagram and YouTube this year, next year, when you leave school, or whether you carry on using it in secret – follow my tips below for staying happy online. The internet has made me feel unhappy many, many times and I want you to learn from my mistakes and be able to enjoy it.

When I was your age, my friends and I used an instant messaging service to talk after school. I'd get home, have a snack, switch on my computer . . . and straight away the arguing would start. People would gossip, pick on others, cyberbully and start fall-outs over nothing. It's hard to tell someone's tone when they are typing and people can often take something the wrong way. My friends and I argued so much more online than we ever did in person! My mum used to despair and say, "That thing [social media] causes so many problems!" and she was right, it did. Now that social media has grown so huge, cyberbullying and 'trolling' – when somebody, often a stranger, goes out of their way to say bad things about you and to you online – is commonplace. People will say things when they are at home on their phones or computers that they wouldn't say to an actual human being stood in front of them. They feel they can get away with horrible comments, and social media gives bullies an easy platform.

This is something I have experienced a lot since becoming a TV presenter. I've had people make comments about my weight, my hair, my makeup, my general appearance. People disagree with what I have posted, or criticise my presenting skills and ability to do my job. It's something which comes with the job, although I don't believe that it should. I have spent entire days crying and feeling sad and worthless because of something someone has said online. I used to search my name on social media to find things people were saying about me, as if I wanted to upset myself. After a while I stopped doing that because I realised that even if ten people said something really nice about me and one person said something mean, I'd ignore all the nice comments and that one sentence – that one insult – would affect me for days. In reality, none of the comments matter – the good ones or the bad ones. All that matters is that you're comfortable with yourself and how you are living your life. You don't know what other people think of you unless they tell you, so I decided that I'm better off not looking for those comments, because someone else's opinion of me shouldn't change my opinion of myself. If I come across someone posting even one mean thing about me, or one mean thing about somebody else (sometimes people get into arguments in the comments section on my pictures!), I block them straight away, and don't waste another second thinking about them.

It's extremely important to be wary of strangers on social media, but sometimes our friends' actions can be dangerous too. I've had friends post pictures and videos of me online that I'd rather weren't there, or had people tactically bully me by posting cryptic statuses or comments about me. I've had friends who have had some terrible experiences online, such as people posting what were private conversations for the whole world to see, and people even setting up entire groups dedicated to bullying somebody. I'm not trying to scare you here – I just want you to be careful about your choices when you're using social media.

You've been through quite a learning curve when it comes to social media, so follow my tips below to ensure that, when you do use it, all will be good.

Love,
Katie xxx

KATIE'S TIPS FOR STAYING HAPPY ON SOCIAL MEDIA!

KEEP YOUR SETTINGS PRIVATE

Only be friends with or allow follows from people you know, trust and like. Have tagging blocks and don't put anything online that you wouldn't want EVERYONE to see – your family, your teachers, your friends, your enemies, the whole school assembly. Trust me, even if you think your account is private, people can find a way to get hold of stuff if they want to, and sometimes there are glitches on social media sites. In a few years' time you'll be glad that nobody else has seen those old selfies you're cringing at! Don't put any personal details like your phone number or address online. In fact, be careful with all your personal information, as people can piece together bits of info to find you – your school name and a picture of you and your friends on your street could be all someone needs. It's easy to be a detective online these days.

BE CAREFUL ABOUT WHAT YOU PUT IN A PHOTO, OR IN WRITING

People have suffered awful unhappiness at the hands of those who they thought were their friends, or boyfriends or girlfriends, when the supposed loyal companion has shared photos of them which they didn't want others to view, or copied and pasted private conversations to somewhere public. People can do mean things like this, intentionally and accidentally, and it's important you protect yourself. Have your most private conversations face to face – it's much safer!

REPORT ANYTHING ONLINE YOU DON'T LIKE

Report anything worrying you to the social media sites themselves. If it's serious, also speak to a parent, teacher or other trusted adult. If a stranger is contacting you, don't respond. If you see a video or picture of something horrible, don't click on it. That kind of thing can really affect your emotions and mental health. You don't want your online experience to be scary and unpleasant. If you feel a bit nervous about something you see or read, there's probably a reason. Trust your instincts and don't look at anything you feel unsure about.

DON'T BELIEVE EVERYTHING YOU SEE ONLINE

Anyone can post anything on the internet. That's why it's so brilliant, but also why it can be a nightmare. If I wanted to, I could write a news article about how I'm marrying a prince and about to be a member of the royal family. There are loads of silly, incorrect news articles, blogs and memes online. There are men who pretend to be teenage girls and teenage girls who pretend to be Justin Bieber and then there's the actual Justin Bieber. There is more Photoshop and fakery than EVER before – don't believe that everyone you follow has a better body than you or more friends or a better life in any way, because you don't know the truth behind the post. People only post what they want others to see – the best bits. You're not seeing their 'behind the scenes', which won't be as glamorous and Insta-worthy.

DON'T SPEND TOO MUCH TIME ONLINE

As fun as it is, and as much as I DO spend quite a lot of time on there, it can be damaging to us. You know how we don't just eat chocolate and chips all day long, because it's bad for our physical health? Well, we must also be in control of habits which could contribute to bad MENTAL health. For example, spending too much time on social media before bed can affect our sleep – that's bad for us. Viewing images of perfect-looking people who are paid to advertise perfect-seeming lives in order to sell products can give us low self-esteem – that's bad for us. Chatting to the mates you have already seen all day at school can lead to gossiping, which leads to arguing, which leads to people getting sick of each other – that's bad for us. Also, if you're online for three hours every night, you're not seeing your family, reading books, playing sports, watching TV, doing your homework, or anything else in those hours – you're missing out on things that will be more beneficial to your life in the long run and bring you greater happiness. You owe it to yourself to look after your mental health and we know that social media can damage it. That doesn't mean you can't use the internet. You just have to moderate it, in the same way you would tell yourself, "I'd better not have that third doughnut." We want the third doughnut, but it will make us unhealthier and unhappier in the long term. So will that third hour on Insta. Limit it – you'll thank yourself for it.

NOTES

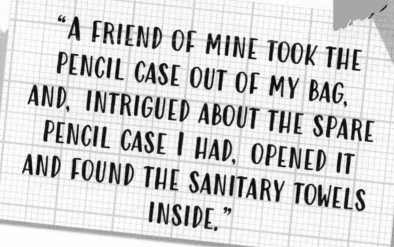

"A FRIEND OF MINE TOOK THE PENCIL CASE OUT OF MY BAG, AND, INTRIGUED ABOUT THE SPARE PENCIL CASE I HAD, OPENED IT AND FOUND THE SANITARY TOWELS INSIDE."

Dear Katie,

My mum left my dad when I was younger and I only ever see her a couple of times a year because she doesn't live near us. I've been learning about periods at school and I'm worried about when I start mine because I'm embarrassed to tell my dad and ask him for sanitary towels from the supermarket.

From Me

Hey You,

Let me start by saying that I'm sorry your mum left and isn't around very much – that must be really hard on you, and I almost want to chat to you about that as well, to make sure you're OK, but you've written to me specifically about periods so I'm going to focus on that. But if there are times when you feel sad about what has happened with your parents, please do ask for help – it's understandable that you might sometimes find that tough to deal with.

For some reason, we all find our periods super-embarrassing when we're young. I did. So did all my friends. It's silly when you think about it, because it's as normal as having ears. It happens to 50% of the population! I'm sure your dad is fully aware of the fact that you will be starting your period soon, and he will also be aware that it's his responsibility to ensure you're happy and healthy. Part of this involves making sure you have the correct sanitary equipment you need when you start menstruating. I suggest you help him do this ahead of time – so whenever there's an appropriate occasion to accompany him to the supermarket, or add sanitary products to the shopping list, or write him a note. Explain that you want to be prepared for when it does happen. It's a part of life that we can't avoid.

I remember the day I started my period. I came home from school and my mum was at work, so I emailed her and in the subject line wrote: "VERY PRIVATE AND CONFIDENTIAL EMAIL!!!!" because I was terrified one of her work colleagues would see it. I wrote it in an email rather than calling her, so that I could avoid saying the words "I've started my period" out loud. The worst possible thing I could have imagined would have been anyone other than my mother knowing about it. Now, on reflection as an adult, that seems really silly, and I find it funny that I was so embarrassed about something which all the other women in my mum's office would have been experiencing as a part of life for many years. I believe it's important that we talk about it though. I have only recently started to admit that my period sometimes makes me feel unwell. But now I do so in front of men as well as women, because we don't need to be treating the fact we have ovaries as a taboo subject and something shameful. Sadly, there will always be some people who do find it awkward and embarrassing, but just because they act uncomfortable about periods doesn't mean you have to.

There may be questions you have about periods which you don't want to ask your dad or that your dad might not know the answer to, but he's not the only person you can go to for advice, and nor is your mum. I'm pleased you've been learning about periods at school, because even though my mum did teach me about them, I also learned a lot of what I know from magazines, books, school and friends. You can do this too. I went to a same-sex girls' school, and while it wasn't perfect, they were excellent at teaching us about periods. It felt like every other day a sanitary towel or tampon company would come in to give out freebies and educate us on the fascinating world of the menstrual cycle. I remember one representative suggesting that, to avoid embarrassment, we keep our sanitary products in a pencil case so that no one knew what they were, and to have some ready in our bag for when we needed them. So I bought a pencil case especially for this and kept all my sanitary freebies in it. Towels, spare knickers, wet wipes – all the things the lady from the company had suggested. I remember being mortified one day when a friend of mine took the pencil case out of my bag, and, intrigued about the spare pencil case I had, opened it and found the sanitary towels inside. I don't know why I found this embarrassing – both of us would end up with periods at some point. Yet such a big deal was made of starting periods, and we'd chat at break times about who had and hadn't 'become a woman' yet. We would worry about whether our sanitary towels were showing through our school skirts or trousers and would ask our friends to walk behind us to check. We'd cough when closing the sanitary bin lid so the person next door didn't hear. And experiencing a 'leak' – our period ending up visible on our clothes – was the worst thing we could possibly imagine. (Even though it happens to everyone at some point and is easily fixed by tying your school jumper around your waist to hide it.)

When you grow up and your female friends have all been having a period every month for years and years, all the worrying you did when you were younger will seem so unnecessary. It feels like a huge thing, getting your period, but believe me, it's all going to be fine.

Your school may or may not educate you about periods as much as mine did, but even if they don't, I'm certain there will be people either at your school or outside of school who can help answer your questions about periods. Find a trusted adult – a teacher, school counsellor, nurse, friend's mum, or an older sibling. Choose a woman if you'd feel more comfortable and confident speaking to a female about these things. You might feel able to pop your mum an email, and ask her the questions you have (although I wouldn't recommend using such a dramatic subject line as I did!). Perhaps she might also be able to broach the subject with your dad?

You might feel a bit awkward the first time you ask your dad for sanitary products, but after that, it will become just another item on the regular shopping list, on there with bananas and orange juice and fabric softener and kitchen towel. It's part of life. You could even show your dad this letter as a means of explaining.

Love,
Katie xxx

DR RADHA'S GUIDE TO PUBERTY

Puberty is a series of changes your body goes through when you're a teenager, to prepare yourself for adulthood.

Puberty is triggered when your body starts producing hormones (chemical messengers) that act on different parts of your body to produce physical changes. These hormones are different for boys and girls – the main hormone driver for boys is testosterone and for girls it is oestrogen. It addition to the physical changes, there are also emotional effects, so it can be a really difficult time. You can get mood swings, feel like you have low self-esteem and sometimes feel angry or low. Puberty normally lasts for about four years.

PUBERTY FOR BOYS
- Average age it starts is twelve years, but can start as early as nine or as late as fourteen
- Testicles get bigger
- Penis starts to grow
- Pubic hair and underarm hair develop

- Wet dreams start
- Sweat more and often develop acne
- Growth spurt and become more muscular
- Voice gets deeper, 'breaks'

PUBERTY FOR GIRLS
- Average age it starts is eleven years, but it can start as early as eight or as late as thirteen
- Breasts start to develop
- Periods start about two years after puberty starts
- Pubic hair and underarm hair develop
- Sweat more and often develop acne
- Growth spurt and body shape changes to have wider hips, and more body fat on thighs, upper back and upper arms

A NOTE ON GENDER
Gender identity is the gender (male or female) that we feel most like or can relate to, whereas 'biological sex' is something we are assigned when we are born according to our genitalia (private parts), chromosomes or hormones. These can be the same but they can also be different. If you feel your biological sex is different from the gender you feel most comfortable as, then it is really good to chat it through with an adult you trust so you can get the support you need to be you.

QUESTIONS YOU ASKED ABOUT PUBERTY, ANSWERED BY DR RADHA!

Q: Does puberty make you hairy on your private parts?
A: Yes – you will develop pubic hair on your private parts. This hair is different from the hair on the top of your head as it is coarser and curlier.

Q: Is it only boys who hit puberty?
A: Both girls and boys go through puberty – some features are the same like mood swings and sweating more, but lots are different.

Q: Why do we have puberty and periods?
A: To prepare your body for adulthood and ultimately to be able to have babies if you want – but only when you are physically and emotionally ready for this.

Q: Does it do anything to your body?
A: Yes there are lots of changes. See page 216.

Q: Does your period hurt?
A: You can get period pains, which feel like crampy pains and spasms in your lower tummy. These normally happen when you start your period. Most of the time they are manageable with a hot water bottle and can get better with gentle exercise. If they are very painful or unmanageable then see your GP who can help. It is

very normal to have periods that are more painful and irregular when they first start, and then they normally settle down.

Q: Why don't boys get a period?
A: Periods happen when an egg is not fertilised by a sperm. The lining of the womb (made up of blood) is no longer needed for a fertilised egg to implant into, and so it's shed and released in a bleed. This all happens in the female reproductive organs which is why people with male reproductive organs don't get periods.

Q: Sometimes I get angry at my friends or cry for no reason. What can I do about my mood swings?
A: Mood swings are part and parcel of puberty and so accepting that they are normal may help. Talk to an adult you trust about how you feel and find ways to get your feelings out like writing, singing, dancing, exercising or drawing. Find ways that help you feel better.

Q: I find it hard at school when I'm on my period. Sometimes teachers don't let us go to the toilet. How can my school life be better with my period?
A: Periods are something that a lot of people in your school and class will be dealing with. Find a quiet moment and let your teacher know you have started

your period and ask if it is OK to use the bathroom if you ask. Experiment with different types of period products – some people feel more comfortable using pads, some use tampons, and some use reusable menstrual cups or specially designed period underwear! Try out different options or brands to find the one that makes you feel most comfortable – this might be different depending on which day of your period you're on. Sport and exercise can help you feel better during your period so try and do what you can. Eating well and getting good sleep can also help.

Q: How can you hide bad smells when you're on your period?

A: Most of the time you're probably worried about a smell that isn't even there. Bad smells can happen from not changing your pads or tampons regularly enough though, so make sure for your own safety and health you are following the instructions on the pack and change them as advised. Always make sure you remove tampons and wash your hands before changing and afterwards. Having regular baths or showers is also really important.

> ## "IN A ROOM FULL OF GIRLS I ALWAYS FELT LIKE THE FRUMPY WEIRDO SURROUNDED BY SUPERMODELS."

Dear Katie,

My friends are all thin and beautiful and everybody loves them.

I'm a gymnast too. All the time, all around me, are just thin pretty girls in leotards – there's no escaping it. All the time, all I see is thin, thin, thin, and I can't get it out of my head.

So before the Christmas holiday I set myself a goal.

Over the Christmas holidays I would put a limit on how much food I would eat and how many calories I intake a day. I've lasted almost the whole holiday just eating dinner (if that), running on 500 calories a day, and my New Year's resolution is to lose as much weight as I can.

My goal for next month is to lose another stone. I've already lost a stone and a half over the holidays, which was originally my goal. But I still don't feel like it's good enough. I'm scared. I know that this stuff is addictive – I've cut myself in the past and have been unable to stop since.

I'm worried that this is going to take me ove, and yet I love doing it. It's too confusing and I'm scared. What do I do?

From Me

Hey You,

Please, let's set a new goal together.

Forget about the old goal. Let's make your new goal to learn how to deal with your emotions healthily.

I don't need to tell you that restricting your calories to

so few and cutting yourself are examples of unhealthy ways of dealing with emotions. You already know that, from what you said in your letter. It's the reason you've written to me.

It isn't surprising that you 'love doing it', because it gives you a sense of control in what can sometimes feel like a chaotic and uncontrollable life. We all want to feel this sense of power over our existence, because we live in fear of what we can't control. You're not alone in wanting to feel like this. People have different ways of dealing with life and making themselves feel better. Many people exercise this control with eating habits or self-harm. In fact, unhealthy eating habits are themselves a form of self-harm.

But there are ways in which you can gain control of your life and emotions healthily, without the guilt and worry that you are doing something very harmful, which I can tell you must be feeling now. This is only replacing your negative emotions with more of the same, and isn't the answer.

I understand how you feel about your body and your friends. I want to reach my arms out of the book and hug you tight, because I hate that you feel this way – I hate that so many of us do. I wish we didn't waste our time worrying about our body sizes and shapes and comparing them to others, but we do. Millions of us do.

Yet, if you were to see those girls in your gymnast class the way they saw themselves, I bet you wouldn't see 'thin, thin, thin' – you'd see all the things they hate about themselves.

I hated my body all of my teens. I can't remember a time when I liked it, a time when I strutted around confidently in a bikini on holiday. In a room full of girls I always felt like the frumpy weirdo surrounded by supermodels. People probably didn't know I felt like this because I hid it well, but here's the truth: I'd be lying if I said I don't still have days now when I feel like that. I look back at pictures of my body when I was younger and long for it. "Ha, I wish I was as fat as I was the first time I thought I was fat!" I laugh miserably, while looking at nineteen year-old Katie on holiday with her mates.

There are days when I think a lot about how unhappy I am with my body, and I feel exhausted with it, and then I'm angry with myself for wasting so much energy on it. If I didn't give a hoot about my body and spent all that time thinking about something worthwhile, perhaps I could be a genius. Imagine what we might be able to achieve if all that time spent hating ourselves, crying in front of mirrors, counting calories, scrolling through Instagram bodies and comparing our own to them was spent doing something worthwhile?

I have been in that room, looking round at my friends/colleagues, and just seeing 'thin, thin, thin'. I've never been a gymnast, but I've done dance and drama and I now work in TV. These are industries, like gymnastics, where people are often body obsessed. For this reason, not only do a lot of people look thin, but the focus on body image and appearance is in the air, in the water – a viral infection of self-obsession that everyone's caught. I've been caught in the trap of using my own and other girls' bodies like it's some sort of game. The mentality of: 'she's got a six pack but at least I've got bigger boobs'. It's total nonsense. Female life does not need to be the big beauty pageant we sometimes turn it into.

Let's go back to your new goal: get better at dealing with my emotions healthily.

You can make a start on this by focusing on your other goals and everything that makes you happy. Try my exercise chart on page 79, but seek help if you need more support – contact a doctor or counsellor and speak to them about what you're doing and how you're feeling. The mind can be mended. Mine has been mended before, and I'm sure it will need mending again before I'm done with this life.

Losing more weight won't make you happy. You know this, based on hard evidence – you reached your original weight loss goal, the one you thought would be good enough, but it wasn't. It wasn't good enough for your mind, which wants to maintain control. You can give it the control it needs in a different way – by learning how to make yourself feel good without self-harming. It's the same, but different. You can do it and you will feel amazing for it. Reaching other happier goals will give you that same feeling you get when you manage to go without dinner – that feeling of achievement and having bettered yourself – without the added dread and fear that comes with knowing you've done something bad for you, which in the long run will cause you more harm and unhappiness.

Good luck with your new goal. A massive hug from me.

Love,
Katie xxx

THERAPIST SALLY SAYS

We all spend time checking how we look – taking care of our bodies is usually a healthy thing to do, but sometimes we feel unrealistically unhappy with what we see and become fixated and upset. We can become so focused on imagined or minor imperfections that we can't stop checking or obsessing about how we look. This behaviour is called body dysmorphic disorder or BDD. It is a condition that involves a wrong idea of how our body looks, and can cause distressing, negative thoughts about our shape, how tall or short, fat or thin we are. It's a kind of imagined ugliness. If you or someone you know has BDD, the first step is recognising what might be the cause. Usually the answer means working on your thoughts, not your looks. BDD can be treated by therapists and doctors.

We all eat for different reasons. Sometimes we eat not because we're hungry, but because we feel really bad. We're bored, lonely, angry or unhappy and rather than deal with the feelings, we turn to food. At other times we want to reward ourselves with a sweet treat or a pizza. Try working out what are the emotional triggers that make you want to eat when you're not hungry. Find a replacement activity. Pause before you reach for the fridge.

On the other hand, sometimes we don't eat because we want to be in control and are obsessed with having a perfect body shape – we're convinced we weigh too much, so we restrict our food, over-exercise or fast and obsessively count calories. Sometimes we eat and then make ourselves sick.

Eating too much or not enough both lead to physical and emotional problems. In both cases we need to find other ways of dealing with situations. Learning to be comfortable with how we are is really important. If you think you have an eating disorder, talk to someone or see your GP.

DR RADHA SAYS

There are many different types of eating disorders, including anorexia nervosa, bulimia, and binge eating disorder. An eating disorder happens when someone's attitude to food becomes distorted and this leads to a change in eating habits. Eating disorders are not only linked to mental well-being and mental health conditions but also to physical health problems.

Anorexia is restricting eating in order to lose weight. People suffering from anorexia often view themselves as overweight even when they are in fact underweight. Anorexia results in hair loss, dry skin, headaches, dizziness, fine hair growing on the body, feeling cold and tired. Long term effects include period problems, fertility problems, osteoporosis (fragile bones), heart problems, pregnancy complications, damage to nerves and organs like liver and kidney.

Bulimia is a cycle of binging (eating a large amount of food in a short amount of time) and then purging (attempting to make yourself sick or using medications to make you poo more). Some of the physical effects include irregular periods, swollen salivary glands, dry skin and brittle fingernails, chemical imbalances in your body and bowel and heart problems.

Binge eating disorder is characterized by episodes of uncontrollable and excessive overeating. Some of the long term effects are obesity, a greater risk of diabetes, heart problems, osteoarthritis and some types of cancer.

NOTES

> ## "SOMETIMES OUR LIVES GET SO COMPLICATED THAT THOSE COMPLICATIONS STOP US FROM BEING GOOD FRIENDS, DAUGHTERS, SONS, FATHERS OR MOTHERS."

Dear Katie,

I hate my mum. She doesn't understand me, she's too strict and she's always interfering with who I'm friends with. She also thinks I'm lying all the time, even when I'm not, so we have big fights and I end up crying in my room for hours on end. I feel really horrible talking about it because I know I'm meant to really like her and be grateful for everything she's done for me. When I tried to talk to someone they just told me I was being a teenager, but I just feel like I'm on my own all the time and I'm so confused. We used to get on when I was little, but I think it's only because I did what I was I told and I acted like she told me to act. She tells me I have to get straight As and then when I get worried about whether I'll be able to do it, she tells me I'm being a nightmare to live with. All my friends are really lucky and get on with their mums. Is there something wrong with me? Am I just a bad person for hating my mum? I'm desperate to talk about how I'm feeling with teachers and my friends' mums, but I feel like a loser and I don't really know what to say.

From Me

Hey You,

Parent and child relationships are complicated. You don't need to feel 'horrible' about talking about your hatred for your mum. There's no written rule which says we must like our parents unconditionally – that simply isn't possible. Some people have dreadful mothers. Some people have amazing mothers. Even the most wonderful mums aren't perfect. Neither are dads, aunties, uncles, grandparents, teachers or any of the other authority figures in your life. They might be older and have more life experience than you, but they are still people.

From time to time, we clash and fall out with lots of people in our lives: parents, children, siblings, friends, boyfriends and girlfriends, colleagues. This is because we are all different and thinking about ourselves, ultimately. Sometimes we don't like it when people aren't behaving in the way we would, or how we want them to, to benefit us. Sometimes we deflect our own issues on to others and sometimes others do that to us. Sometimes our lives get so complicated that those complications stop us from being good friends, daughters, sons, fathers or mothers.

This is most likely what is happening with you and your mum. You both have your own stuff going on and it's complicating your relationship. You don't always agree, and you're clashing because you both really care about each other and want the other to do exactly what YOU want, but that might not be what the other wants. Can you both learn to appreciate your differences and know that, even if you disagree wildly, both opinions are OK?

For example, your mum wants you to get straight As, and you might want that too, but you don't want that pressure put on you or to feel you're good enough if you don't get them. That's understandable. She wants to dictate who you're friends with, but you want to make those decisions yourself – that's understandable too. It's wonderful that your mum wants you to get good grades and hang around with good people, and this shows that she cares about you. This doesn't mean that she knows best. Sometimes she might be right, sometimes she might be wrong.

The best way to tackle something like this is by communicating with your mum. Sometimes things can get hysterical, and the crying, shouting, door-slamming moments aren't those in which issues get resolved. Instead, try approaching your mum when she has some time, and is in a seemingly positive mood, and tell her you're worried about the pressure she's putting on you. Find the same sort of moment to explain to her that you want to make your own mind up about your friends, and again to tell her that it upsets you when she accuses you of telling lies. This might be a pretty terrifying prospect, and you may want to tackle each thing separately, but talking calmly is always a better plan than an anger-fuelled argument. I think your mum will respect you for having a grown-up conversation with her. Go into the conversation with the confidence that all you are doing is telling your mum how you feel, and know that you will feel better for trying to communicate with her in this way.

When I was in my final year of primary school I had a best friend who was going through a tough time at home. Because of this, she wasn't exactly a model student at school. At the parents' evening, one of my teachers told my mum that she should stop me from being friends with her, because she might be a bad influence on me.

The teacher and my mum meant well – they only wanted what was best for me – but in this instance they were wrong. On this particular issue I knew better. I knew the friend was having a hard time but, if anything, was actually a very positive influence on me. She was emotionally intelligent, caring and loving, and looked after me as much as I looked after her. She wanted the best for me, just like my teacher and mum did, and she wouldn't have done anything to negatively influence my life. We're still friends now. My mum believed me when I told her this – she must have seen the determination in my face when I insisted my friend was a positive part of my life.

But parents and their children don't always agree, and sometimes agreeing to disagree, although frustrating, might be the only answer. You don't need to change your mind or opinions, but accept that some compromises need to be made on both sides for you and your mum to have a happier relationship.

Your mum might have her own stuff going on too. Sometimes we find it hard to imagine our guardians also need guidance at times. Can you arrange some quality time with your mum? Ask her questions about her and how she is? Start a conversation about her teenage years – her friends and her exams and so on – and it might help you to understand each other and take her back to when she was a teen, to encourage her to empathise with you.

Love,
Katie xxx

THERAPIST SALLY SAYS

Here's a surprising thought: Perhaps the opposite of love isn't hate – it's fear. We often confuse anger with hate. Work out what you're angry about, deal with your anger and then talk to your mum.

"IT'S A BEAUTIFUL THING WHEN YOU REALISE THAT JUST BEING YOURSELF IS GOOD ENOUGH, AND THAT YOU DON'T HAVE TO CHANGE TO FIT IN WITH ANYONE."

Dear Katie,

What's your advice for someone who feels like they don't fit in with the 'norm'? Have you ever experienced it, and how did you overcome it?

I've always felt like I don't fit in within a group of friends, like I'm a little bit weird. I've been thinking about it a lot recently. I was wondering if you think everyone feels that they don't fit in – is it just a mind game we play with ourselves? Is there ever a way we can fully accept who we are?

From Me

Hey You,

Your question is brilliant – and your answer is right there in your letter. I'm pretty sure that everyone thinks they don't fit in – at least at some point in their lives.

I haven't ever felt like I've fully fitted in. I don't even understand what it means, if I'm honest. How can you fully 'fit in' with everyone when we're all different?

Teenagers have always formed certain groups. They're called 'youth subcultures' and are often defined by music taste and fashion. In the 1920s there were dandies and flappers, and in the 1950s and 1960s there were teddy boys, mods, rockers and hippies. When I was at school there were goths and moshers. Maybe at the time you're reading this book, people identify as emos, or hipsters, or beliebers. Some people assign themselves to these subcultures and their identity is defined. There seems to be a set of rules about fitting in to them – a certain hairstyle or jacket or choice of vehicle.

Like you, I have often worried about whether or not I fit in. My group of school friends were all so different and nowadays we all have extremely varied jobs and lives. Throughout my life I've found myself in different groups – at school, college, university, at various different jobs, in my family. And in every group I will have questioned my place in it and whether I'm worthy.

But it's a beautiful thing when you realise that just being yourself is good enough, and that you don't have to change to fit in with anyone. I used to give myself a hard time if I hadn't seen a certain TV show that my friends were obsessing about, or visited a certain place or listened to a certain album or bought clothes from a certain shop or had a certain hobby. I'd try so hard to fit in and keep up with all these things. Looking back, I must have been a bit annoying, desperately trying to impress the various groups I was in, and probably not managing to successfully achieve anything. Nowadays I'm like, "No, I don't like avocado," "Soz, that musician really isn't my thing," and "No, I tried watching one episode of that TV show, but I can't stand it." Sometimes I like the same things as my friends and colleagues, and sometimes I don't. The difference is that now I admit it and get on with my life, spending little to no time worrying about whether or not that means I 'fit in'. I have friendships which make me happy, with people I have stuff in common with, yet we are also different in many ways – but I have myself and I'm comfortable with that and, do you know what? It's such a relief not to have to try so hard any more!

Because what is 'fitting in' anyway? What are we trying

to fit into? A pair of skinny jeans? One of those little smart cars?

I don't think you need to change yourself to try to fit in because that isn't who you are. You are you – you are what you like and what you dislike. You are your experiences and memories and passions and goals. You don't have to be a goth or a hipster or a geek or a flapper (although it would be pretty cool if you brought back the flapper subculture all by yourself – those gals knew how to dress). You are YOU and you're not basic or boring or weird or anything – you're an individual like everyone else.

I like listening to Radio 4 and going to literature festivals but I also like watching reality TV and taking selfies. I used to think I couldn't mix up those things – that I was either one type of person or the other. I used to try really hard to be like the people around me, but then I realised that the happy ones were just being themselves. I decided I wanted that confidence too.

Drop the idea of fitting in and instead focus on having fun with your friends. Admit you like or don't like something even if it's the opposite of what your friends think. Be yourself. It will be like a huge sigh of relief leaving your lungs – like you've stopped living a lie. You don't need to be anyone else but you.

Trust me, it's much more interesting and engaging when people don't care about fitting in.

Love,
Katie xxx

NOTES

_____

_____

_____

_____

_____

_____

_____

_____

_____

_____

_____

_____

_____

_____

_____

_____

> ## "WE GET BY, WE GATHER LIFE EXPERIENCES AND THEN WE LEARN TO FLY ON OUR OWN."

Dear Katie,

I am worried about growing up – if I'll get a job, if I'll get a house, if I'll be able to afford to feed my family. I am ten years old, and I don't want to talk to anyone about this worry because I feel embarrassed. I am worried about getting ill or getting old and not being able to do the fun things I do now. I am also worried because I want to make my parents proud of me. I feel like they might think that I don't always care for them, but I do.

From Me

Hey You,

I understand why you feel embarrassed about the prospect of talking to someone about your concerns, because people often act like when you're young you shouldn't have problems and you don't have anything to worry about. But that simply isn't true. That's why I'm writing this book.

It's totally understandable to worry about our futures – why wouldn't we? They are, well, our very own futures! We want them to be happy and carefree, but we hear things which make us concerned they might not be – grown-ups talking about the perils of being an adult, items on the news, other people's problems that we've witnessed.

I can guarantee there will be times in your life when you're not entirely happy, when things are making you feel stressed and worn out. No matter what happens during your life, there is a solution to every problem and, most importantly, you will have a choice. You can choose what you do and you can choose how you decide to view situations and circumstances.

Being an adult can be hard, but not as hard as we sometimes like to make out. At the end of the day, it's what we are supposed to be doing. We are meant to grow up and move from being looked after by our parents to looking after ourselves. Just like a baby bird is fed little worms (gross) by its parents before learning to fly, and going off on its own. It's in our nature. We figure it out. We get by, we gather life experiences and then we learn to fly on our own.

You worrying about this clearly indicates that you're going to be sensible about your decisions, making it even more likely you will get a job and have somewhere to live and be able to afford food. What you're already demonstrating is a sense of responsibility – you know that your future is in your hands.

The fact you care so much about your parents that you've written to me to say you're worried they don't know you care, tells me something – that they do know. In any case, go and tell them right now. Put a bookmark in this book or fold over the corner of the page (some people hate that, but I don't mind – to me, books should look like they've been read) and go and tell your parents that you love them and care about them. There's nothing stopping you from doing what you need to do to feel better about your life – right now.

When I'm worrying about the future and all the terrible things that probably won't happen to me, I try to remind myself that I have always worried, my whole life, since your age or maybe even before. Yet everything has always been fine. So far, so good. I have always had a job and been able to afford food. Lots of things I have worried about haven't happened. Some things I have worried about have happened, but I got through them. Get a pen and piece of paper and write down a time that something you'd been worrying about happened. What was it? What was the outcome? Did you get through it? The answer is yes. Did you learn from it, grow from it? How did it change you as a person? Did it make you more resilient or better at making decisions, or somehow shape the person you are today?

Whenever anxiety is getting the better of me, I remind myself that the things I am worried about probably won't happen, and even if they do, I will survive.

So will you.

Love,
Katie xxx

"HAVING A BOYFRIEND DOESN'T PROVE ANYTHING."

Dear Katie,

All my friends have boyfriends, but boys don't like me. They're always mean to me. Last summer this boy asked me out and I said yes and then he went off and laughed with his mates because the whole thing had been a trick. He said, "As if I'd go out with you!' I didn't tell anyone because it was too embarrassing and then all my friends would realise I'm not like them. I feel so ugly. What's wrong with me? I like someone, but he already has a girlfriend, and all his friends tease me. I feel faint and dizzy when I see him but I don't trust any of the boys I know now. I don't think I'll ever get a boyfriend – am I just weird?

From Me

Hey You,

You're not weird, and there's nothing wrong with you.

I used to feel like this too. In fact, although I'm older now and I've had boyfriends and I'm much more confident, I'm still surprised when someone likes me. I'm like: who, me? Me, with this face? But I'm so weird! How can anyone like me?

When I was in primary school I remember feeling so ugly compared to the other girls. They just seemed to be prettier or cooler or more confident, or had something which made other people – boys included – feel drawn to them. I never felt part of that crew. I felt like my skin was pimply and my hair was scruffy and dull. I thought there was nothing particularly interesting about me. I didn't bother trying to talk to any of the cool boys because I decided they were out of my league.

I didn't even want a boyfriend, not really.

We should only want a boyfriend/girlfriend because we want to hang out with someone we like, a lot of the time. When I was worrying about not having a boyfriend, I already had good friendships and I hadn't met a boy I really liked or wanted to spend time with. I just wanted a boyfriend – but not for the right reasons.

I probably wanted a boyfriend because my friends had boyfriends or wanted boyfriends, and I felt as if having a boyfriend proved something – that I was cool, pretty, accepted and as good as the other girls and boys who were dating. Having a boyfriend doesn't actually prove any of that, and when I eventually got one I realised you don't need a boyfriend to feel all these things – you can find that happiness and confidence in yourself. And do you know what the best thing about that is? You're only relying on you. You can have that happiness and confidence regardless of whether you're single or in a relationship with this boy or that boy or if a boy dumps you or you dump a boy or whatever. Do you know what else is great about it? Once you start exuding that confidence, you'll find that not only will YOU like yourself better, but other people will too.

Often when we are feeling really rubbish about ourselves, we find things don't go so well. But if something boosts our confidence and life is good, more great things seem to come. Working on your confidence will make you feel like you don't need anyone else in order to be happy, because you can make yourself feel good. The irony is, that's when boys will start to notice you for who you really are, not who you currently think you are.

Confidence doesn't come overnight and it is an ongoing process. When I was a teenager, I tried all sorts of techniques to improve mine. I'd smile at myself in every mirror I passed (a bit embarrassing when you forget you're not on your own and do it in front of someone!). I'd talk in the mirror and dance in the mirror, practising my conversation and moves for the school disco ahead of time. I started going to a drama club to help improve my confidence. Plus, as well as getting up and putting yourself out there in front of people, it also makes you feel good due to a sense of achievement. AND you meet a whole new group of people you have something in common with, people who you can be whoever you want to be in front of.

There are other ways you can improve your confidence – you can do my activity on page 79 to remind yourself who you are and what makes you you, and don't forget that whoever you are is totally good enough. Fill out your name on page 64 and stick it somewhere to remind you of this every day. You ARE good enough.

Also, remember that friends sometimes lie. A lot of my friends at school pretended they'd had boyfriends when they hadn't. We all bent the truth a little to make it sound like we'd experienced more than we had. We all lied about how many boys we'd kissed or made up imaginary online boyfriends or boys in groups of friends our schoolmates didn't know. Getting a boyfriend or girlfriend can become an obsession amongst groups of young friends. I wouldn't have thought any less of my friends if they'd admitted they'd actually never had a boyfriend. Most of us didn't have proper boyfriends until we left secondary school – I certainly didn't.

You don't need these boys to like you and if they don't, don't give them the time of day. I used to try too hard to impress people because I really, really cared what they thought. I wanted boys to fancy me, girls to like me and colleagues to admire me. I carried on trying to make an effort with people who weren't at all interested for far too long. But you don't need these people. Focus on those who do make an effort to be nice to you and get to know you, and the people who make you feel good. They are the only people who matter and who will enrich your life. Ask yourself: do you like everyone else? I'm sure, like me, you don't! Sometimes we like people and they like us, sometimes we like people and they don't like us, sometimes they like us but we don't like them. It works the other way around – sometimes boys have liked me and I haven't liked them back, but I'm sure they got over it and found someone who does like them. Just as I've found people I like with whom the feeling is mutual!

It's mean what that boy and his friends did to you, but unfortunately sometimes that kind of stuff happens. It's understandable that you feel hurt and rejected, so be nice to yourself about it. I remember the most popular boy in school once asking me if I'd go out with him, and I said "No!" because I was shy and embarrassed and assumed it must have been a joke. Sure enough, he laughed in my face as if to say, "I obviously didn't mean it, spotty." But not everyone is like this, most people aren't mean, so don't let this one incident change how you feel about boys. This boy has clearly got too big for his boots and was showing off in front of his mates. He might actually fancy you, he might not, or he might not fancy anyone yet. His reason for doing this won't have been to single you out or hurt you or because of anything to do with you, but rather to get a laugh and make himself feel better in front of his peers. It will come back to bite him on the bum. He'll learn.

You will get a boyfriend, if and when you want one, but you don't need one to be happy. Work on being you. Loving yourself and being happy in yourself is a superpower.

Love,
Katie xxx

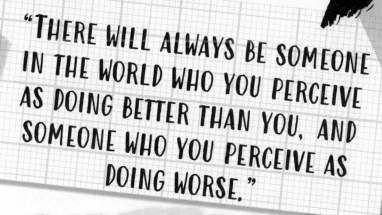

"THERE WILL ALWAYS BE SOMEONE IN THE WORLD WHO YOU PERCEIVE AS DOING BETTER THAN YOU, AND SOMEONE WHO YOU PERCEIVE AS DOING WORSE."

Dear Katie,

My mum and dad don't have a lot of money and can't always buy me the latest trainers or computer games. I am worried about the way I look and the clothes I wear. I don't have all the expensive brands that my friends have. I don't know what to do because I'm worried I will get bullied about it.

From Me

Hey You,

Isn't it strange that we place so much value on brands? On material things? That once upon a time, someone decided that rather than running around with our willies and boobies out, we should put a bit of cloth on them and protect our 'modesty', and then decided that we should probably wear some more cloth, to keep us warm when it's cold, and protected from the sun and the wind and all the other elements. Then someone decided we could get really fun and creative with it and wear different materials and colours and use it to demonstrate who we are and what we like and to feel good about ourselves. Then someone wrote like 'Dave'* on it, gave it a 'name' and charged us loads of money for that same bit of cloth.

It's pretty silly when you think about it, because even though buying clothes and expressing ourselves through what we wear can make us feel happy, there are so many other things that make us happy – things which don't cost us any money. Like people. Other people probably make us happier than anything else in the world. Spending time with friends and family – the ones who make us feel good at least – laughing and joking and talking and cuddling, those are the things that really make us feel good. Think

*I'm not aware that there are any clothing brands called 'Dave'.

about yourself – I bet you haven't judged anyone or liked anyone less because they haven't been wearing a designer brand or didn't have the latest computer game, have you? In fact, I bet you've liked them more for it and that you've only noticed it because you're worried about how people view you. I certainly wouldn't have a better time with my best mate if she was wearing an expensive designer brand than if she was wearing a bin bag. We wouldn't laugh more or have better conversations (in fact, we would definitely laugh a lot more if she was wearing a bin bag).

I doubt you need me to tell you that owning these things won't actually make you happier – because they are just a way of us covering up our insecurities. However, you might need me to tell you that your friends with all the designer clothes and computer games probably feel just as insecure as you. Sure, they have the latest designer hoodie, but then there will be someone else with an even newer one or an even more expensive one. They might have got a new video game for their birthday, but somebody else got two. There's always a bigger fish. There will always be someone in the world who you perceive as doing better than you, and someone who you perceive as doing worse. There are a lot of us, and all our situations are different.

For now, focus on being the person you want to be, the friend you want to be, and the child you want to be to your parents. I'm sure they love you so much and wish they could afford to buy you everything in the world. Make a list of all the things you enjoy doing that don't cost any money – your hobbies, spending time with your friends, reading a library book – and focus on all that. You'll get much more pleasure out of those things than you would out of receiving the latest sought-after item, which will soon be replaced by something newer and supposedly better.

Forget about Dave and his silly designer jeans. No one needs to buy your stupid expensive jeans, Dave.

Love,
Katie xxx

> ## "NO ONE CAN MAKE YOU DO ANYTHING YOU DON'T WANT TO DO."

Dear Katie,

My friends drink alcohol and I don't, but every day after school they tell me to come to the toilets to drink with them. I tried to report this to an adult but they threatened me and say they will harm me if I tell. My friends also often try to dare me to do stuff. I worry about daring. Please can you help me? What can I do?

From Me

Hey You,

When I was in secondary school I was the only one in my group of friends who didn't smoke. My best friends never forced or even encouraged me to smoke because they cared about me, but other people tried to get me to do it. I would sit on the school bus around all the smokers and if people suggested I smoked I refused, confidently and forcefully. I would sit wafting the second-hand smoke out of my face and turning my nose up at it. If someone asked me to try a cigarette I'd say, "Why would I bother trying a cigarette when I don't want to start smoking?" I'd be like, "No thanks, smoking doesn't appeal to me. I don't really get why you all do it, to be honest." I was never picked on for this. My friends might have jokingly called me a goody-two-shoes or talked about 'clean-cut Katie' behind my back, but nobody was ever intentionally mean or bullied me about it. After the first couple of times, nobody tried to get me to do it again.

By giving a firm no, and making it clear I'd made a decision not to smoke, I'd shown people that they couldn't boss me around. The problem with peer pressure, which is what you're talking about in your letter, is that once you give in – once you let somebody get past your protests and make you do something you don't want to do – you've shown them that they have that power over you.

If they are the type of person who likes power or if they want to drag you down with them because they've given into peer pressure themselves, they will carry on and carry on.

I tried not to follow the crowd and to make my own decisions, but of course I wasn't always successful in doing so. It can be very hard to do this when you want to fit in and get on with your friends. When I was a bit older than you I sometimes drank alcohol with my friends at the weekends. I hated the taste of it and hung around with not-so-nice people in the cold and dark on the streets, and at times I felt really unsafe and told my friends that I wanted to go home. I hadn't wanted to go there in the first place, but I'd found it difficult to resist my friends' pressure and I didn't want to feel as though I'd missed out on something. I learned some important lessons, including that I definitely wasn't missing out on anything – hanging around on the streets in the dark with boys in tracksuits, drinking awful, cheap wine was something I wished I had missed. I also learned that your friends don't always make the best decisions, or have your best interests at heart all the time. I don't think my friends particularly enjoyed doing it either and they might not have meant to pressurise me. Maybe they felt that they needed to do these things and wanted safety in numbers – convincing more people to do what they were doing, to justify it to themselves.

If you are friendly but firm, like I was with my smoker friends, you probably won't need to fall out with anyone or tell a teacher. I hope that being your own person and making your own decisions will give you the respect you deserve. But if it doesn't, I suggest you consider separating yourself from these friends and hanging out with some new ones. It can be disappointing when our friends start doing things that we don't approve of, but you can't control them any more than they can control you – everyone has to make their own decisions. You might have to accept that they are going to drink and leave them to it, so you can prioritise your own safety and happiness.

Be your own person.

Love, Katie xxx

"LONELINESS IS A STRANGE THING"

Dear Katie,

I have known my best friend since birth, but now she has moved to a different city and I am feeling lonely and like I have lost her. We can text and FaceTime but it is not the same. What can I do? She is very special to me and we might fall apart because of it.

From Me

Hey You,

I'm sorry to hear that you're feeling lonely. Loneliness is a strange thing because we can feel it even when we are surrounded by people, if we don't have anyone around who understands us or makes us feel comfortable. You knew your friend from birth, and I'm assuming she made you feel good and comfortable and safe. Don't beat yourself up about feeling sad about this. You're grieving because you don't have that person in your life in the same way any more, but you haven't lost her.

Things are going to be different between you and your friend now. Take a deep breath and accept that – say it out loud: "Our friendship is going to change because of the distance." But although it will change, it certainly doesn't need to be over. I hope accepting that makes you feel better – I often feel relieved when I realise the thing I'm worrying about might come true, and start dealing with that and adjusting to the new situation.

When I was eleven, one of my friends went to live in another town an hour away, after her parents split up. We spoke on the phone every single day. During that time I went through a tough period with some friends at school and used to call her every day to tell her all about it. She kept me going and in some ways it was nice to have a friend who was a bit further away, and not part of any of the school dramas that were going on. I could confide in her and find solace in our friendship when day-to-day life was tricky, without worrying that I'd be making things worse. Just before Christmas, my parents agreed to drive me to her house, as we were going to visit someone else nearby. I was going to surprise her and take her a Christmas present. It was a lovely moment between me and my friend when I turned up at her door unannounced – we still talk about it to this day.

My friend still lives an hour away, but when we catch up we always spend good quality time together. We have phone calls which end up lasting hours – no matter how long it's been since we last saw or spoke to each other, it feels like nothing has changed when we get chatting.

That said, it is very different. We haven't been 'there' physically for events in each other's lives. Sometimes it will be a while before we tell the other about something major that's happened. In some ways I'm closer to other friends who live near me and who I see more, but in other ways I'll never be as close to anyone as I am to my oldest friend.

If you both value each other's friendship, I'm certain this will be the case for you. As your friend isn't going to be there for you every day in a physical capacity, try to enjoy spending time with your other friends. If you'd like to make more friends, could you join an after-school club where you'd meet new people?

The fact that you've written to me about this friend you've known from birth to tell me how special she is gives me great faith that you two will always be friends. It's likely that you'll continue to have a lovely friendship, even if it will be in a different way.

Love,
Katie xxx

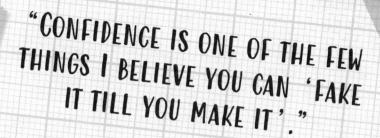

"CONFIDENCE IS ONE OF THE FEW THINGS I BELIEVE YOU CAN 'FAKE IT TILL YOU MAKE IT'."

Dear Katie,

Have you always been confident? If not, when did you begin being confident and how can I help my confidence so I can perform in drama or sing?

From Me

Dear Katie,

How can I be more confident at talking to people? Or talking in front of a crowd? Have you always been this confident? If not, what motivates you to stay calm in front of people? I am not a very confident person and I would like to become more confident.

From Me

Hey Both of You,

Loads of people wrote to me about confidence and you all wanted to know if I have always been confident. The quick answer is DEFINITELY NOT.

In fact, when I was in primary school, I was so shy and quiet that my teachers asked my parents if everything was OK at home. My own dad once said that he can't believe it's the same person when he sees me on telly or on a stage if he thinks back to how I was as a little girl.

I remember being very nervous and timid all through primary school. Then I went to secondary school and something changed. It was almost like someone flipped the 'confident' switch in me, or rather, it was like it suddenly occurred to me that I could be a different person in secondary school. I love that about fresh starts. On induction day I was mostly surrounded by complete strangers, plus one or two people from my primary school who were good friends and nice people. All the people who had intimidated me in primary school were gone and I saw it as a new opportunity. I don't think I even realised I was doing it at the time, but I let the real, silly me come out – the one which usually only my closest friends saw. As an ice-breaker we had to go around the room and take it in turns to come up with a nickname for ourselves using alliteration. We had to say why we'd chosen that name, for example, 'Amazing Abdul' or 'Brilliant Beth' or something. When it got to me, I'd taken my scrunchie out of my ponytail and wrapped it around my head like a bandana with all of my hair sticking up in a funny way. I told everyone in my best American accent that my name was Kit Kat Katie because I liked Kit Kats. I know, it sounds like the most unfunny, cringeworthy thing ever, but for some reason everyone found it funny and started to like me. I kept doing accents, mostly American, and people called me 'American girl'. I was weird. But I was confident and popular, for a while anyway.

Then I had a big falling out with some friends and endured a year of bullying, and my confidence took a complete nosedive. I remember going through a phase where I couldn't speak to anyone without blushing. I didn't want to answer questions in class and I was only confident when I was in charge of a situation – for example, when messing around with my remaining couple of mates at lunchtime. I'd become shy and embarrassed if anyone I didn't know spoke to me, or if someone started a conversation unexpectedly.

My confidence went up and down and up and down depending on my situation, because I allowed people around me to influence it. When surrounded by people who made me feel comfortable I flourished, and when bullied I shrank to a shadow of the class-clown version of me.

Nowadays I've figured out who I am (not American – I can't do any accents any more!). I'm confident around most people and in most situations. There are a couple of ways in which I've achieved that, which I'll tell you about now, but I also think that confidence grows with time, so be patient with yourself.

I'm much more confident now because I've spent so much time public speaking and presenting, so I'm very used to it. That doesn't mean I don't get nervous and shy still – I just hide it well by 'faking it'! Confidence is one of the few things I believe you can 'fake it till you make it'. If you pretend you're confident about something, your brain becomes convinced of it, and before you know it you're public speaking, or chatting to your crush, or acting silly in a play. To the outside world you appear totally calm – in fact, even YOU think you're cool. Celebrities often talk about having an on-screen persona – sometimes they give this person a name, and imagine they are being this completely different, confident person when they're performing. That's one trick I think really works.

The second way is to throw yourself out of your comfort zone and into something which demands confidence. For example, I went to a drama club during my first few years of secondary school and that really helped. My current job has forced me to be confident.

Try joining a club if you want to improve your confidence – but only something you want to do and will enjoy. Ultimately our confidence comes from how comfortable we feel within ourselves – often we are not confident because we're worried about how people will perceive us. The only way to truly feel confident is to 'own it'. Accept the person you are, forget about what other people think and remember that only YOUR opinion of yourself matters. Remind yourself of all the things that are good about you. Don't be ashamed about any part of your personality. Get to know yourself – figure out who you are. Remember that you don't need to be the loud, confident class clown – that doesn't make you a better or more interesting person. Just be yourself and enjoy yourself.

Love,
Katie xxx

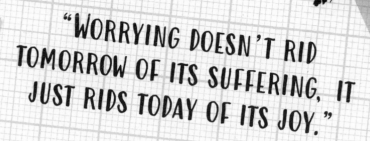

"WORRYING DOESN'T RID TOMORROW OF ITS SUFFERING, IT JUST RIDS TODAY OF ITS JOY."

Dear Katie,

I am concerned because my mum and dad are arguing and I don't want them to split up. I know people whose parents have divorced and I don't want that to happen to my mum and dad too. I don't know what to do!

From Me

Hey You,

When I was at school I was the only person in my friendship group whose parents hadn't split up, and I used to really worry about it too.

Most of us are guilty of worrying about things which might never happen. Your parents arguing doesn't necessarily mean they're going to split up – people often argue when they are in relationships. Sometimes it doesn't mean anything other than they're going through a bit of a difficult time and are disagreeing about life's decisions. I can't comment on your parents' relationship as I don't know them, but there are two important points to remember: (1) there's no evidence to say your parents are definitely going to split up, and (2) even if they do, you will survive. Say that out loud: "I will survive. I will survive." You can even sing the song if you want to (you know the one, I'm sure!).

I suggest you speak to your parents – sit them both down together and tell them how you've been feeling. I'm sure they love you and you're their main priority. They will most likely tell you that they're not going to spilt up and that you don't need to worry. Talking to your parents may help them to communicate better between each other and put them on the path to fixing the arguing problem. So don't be afraid to talk – communication is key in every relationship. I believe many problems could be solved if people spoke to those they loved calmly and honestly rather than putting it off and burying their heads in the sand.

Your family will exist whether your parents divorce or not. Whatever happens, family bonds are a powerful thing and even if the structure changes, your parents will always be your family.

Love,
Katie xxx

NOTES

> ## "WE SEE OUR SIBLINGS AT THEIR VERY BEST AND THEIR VERY WORST — AND THEY SEE US THAT WAY TOO."

Dear Katie,

My brother is always horrible to me. My parents tell me to ignore him hitting me and at night-time he watches videos on his phone so I can't sleep – I can't even sleep with a clock in my room. He calls me names like 'gay' and so I'm asking you how I deal with that.

From Me

Dear Katie,

I always make fun of my brother and sister. They don't like it, then they tell my mum and I get in a lot of trouble or grounded.

From Me

Hey Both of You,

I'm going to answer your letters together, so that you can both see the struggles on each side.

Our relationships with our siblings are complex. Often we have this wonderful idea about what it should be like – our family members should all get on in perfect harmony, our siblings should be ready-made friends, our family should always be there for us. It can be extremely disappointing when that doesn't happen – when they're very different to us, annoying, imperfect or distant – because we don't think this is the way it should be.

Most people would admit they take their bad moods out on the people closest to them. We might be lovely to people all day at work or school but then come home and be moody, irritating, sharp and perhaps even nasty to the people in our family, because we trust that they are always going to be there. Our friends might cut us out of their lives if we behaved like that towards them, but siblings are less likely to.

This means we see our siblings at their very best and their very worst – and they see us that way too. Outside of our family we often hide our less desirable traits such as anger, jealousy and greed. The question is, can we accept that we're both good and bad, lovely and horrid – in others and ourselves?

To the first letter: it sounds like you have already complained to your brother and parents about his behaviour and it hasn't changed anything. Your folks are probably telling you to ignore it because they think it is just innocent sibling tormenting. They are most likely irritated by it themselves and just want you to get along. It might be innocent banter, but it might not.

I have a friend I've known since primary school whose brother made fun of her and fought with her when we were very young. It started with him hiding her dolls and sneaking up on her in scary masks, but when we were teenagers I witnessed him calling her terrible names and telling her she was pathetic and ugly and would never get a boyfriend. I knew these things really hurt her. I recently caught up with this old friend and as we chatted about our families she told me that she didn't see much of her brother these days and that their relationship, though better, wasn't the best. She'd come to realise that all his tormenting wasn't just a bit of innocent 'sibling banter' but actual sibling bullying. It had affected their relationship and contributed to the insecurities she felt as a young woman. We sometimes don't realise that what seems like innocent jibes can change the way we feel about ourselves and affect our confidence long-term. For this reason, we must be kind to ourselves and avoid those who aren't kind to us, or intervene to stop their hurtful actions.

Try talking to your brother or parents again, and this time be very clear that it isn't innocent teasing but something which is seriously affecting you. And if they don't pay attention, could you speak to another family member such as an aunt, uncle or older cousin?

(Also, about the clock – I totally get it. When I was being bullied at school I suffered terribly with insomnia and the slightest noise kept me awake, clocks especially. WHY ARE THEY SO ANNOYING?)

To the second letter: ask yourself why you want to make fun of your brother and sister. How does it make you feel when you do it? Do you feel in control, less angry? What does it do to you? Slow down and ask yourself: what is it that I need in this moment? Attention? Are you feeling jealous? Competitive? In need of a hug or someone to hang out with? Are you 'testing' what it is like to be mean to someone, and seeing how they react?

How do you feel when you don't make fun of your brother and sister?

I'm sure you don't need me to tell you why your mum tells you off about this. Presumably your brother and sister don't like it and they complain and protest. The conflict might be annoying or upsetting for your mum and she wants you to get along. Perhaps she's worried that you making fun of your siblings could make them unhappy, because it could.

Thinking about why we do the things we do can help us to make informed decisions about how we want to treat others, and ourselves. Often when people are mean, it isn't to do with the person they are inflicting that on, but concerned with something they are going through themselves.

Love,
Katie xxx

NOTES

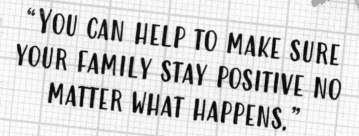

"YOU CAN HELP TO MAKE SURE YOUR FAMILY STAY POSITIVE NO MATTER WHAT HAPPENS."

Dear Katie,

My parents are in their overdraft a lot. Their mattress is making their backs ache every morning. Their selflessness of taking my family on a Christmas holiday has come at a cost.

From Me

Hey You,

I'm sorry to hear that you're worrying about your family's finances.

It is quite common for people to be in their overdraft, so don't worry too much about this. It's happened to me lots of times in my adult life. Overdraft is a very boring term which refers to an amount of money a bank allows you to use after you use up the money you actually had in your back account. Most people don't know about it until they're adults, when a bank allows your account to have this feature. I'm assuming you must have heard your parents talking and that has got you worried.

But as their child, this isn't for you to sort out. The best way for you to help the situation is by enjoying your time with your family and having fun and smiling and laughing and doing all the things you always did. You don't need to be on holiday or to spend money to have fun with your family. Can you devote more time to watching TV with them, reading with them, helping them with cooking or cleaning, organising a games night or going for walks? You can help to make sure your family stays positive no matter what happens – because bank balances fluctuate and good and bad times come and go. The things that make us happy remain the same and have done so since the beginning of time. Surveys on happiness often show that as long as a person is financially comfortable, they are no less happy than a millionaire or a billionaire. As long as we have food and a roof over our heads and all our basic needs met, anything extra doesn't bring us any more happiness, even if we sometimes think it would.

Speak to your parents and tell them you're worried – they might be able to put your mind at rest and give you a big cuddle.

Love,
Katie xxx

NOTES

"DON'T BE AFRAID TO LIVE ON PLANET MY MUM DIED."

Dear Katie,

I am thirteen years old and last year I lost the most precious person, my mother. I am worried that my problems at home will make me work less hard in school. When I come to school I think my friends will help me feel better, but they don't. They moan about how much they hate their parents and this makes me feel even worse. I feel let down by the people I love the most and I wish I had my mother to heal the pain.

From Me

Hey You,

It isn't fair that you had to lose your mother so young. My parents are incredibly special to me, as your mother was to you, and I've often thought about what I will do when they die, and how I will keep going. People grieve in different ways and you must find what works for you. You shouldn't compare yourself to anyone else or worry about the rate at which you are feeling better or the time it takes for you to get back on track at school. Do whatever you need and want to do, because your situation is completely individual – yes, there are other people who have lost their mothers at your age, but every single one of those situations is unique. I have friends who have lost their mothers, and they've all coped with their grief in different ways – had counselling, had a tattoo in memory of their mum, made photo montages and collages of the happy times they shared, wrote a diary of letters addressed to their mother. Grief is very individual, and you must do whatever you need to do to keep the memory of your mum and work through your feelings of loss. As you grieve, you can still get on with your own life, because you are young and you have a wonderful life ahead of you.

Focus on the things that make you feel good and happy, while remembering it's OK to let yourself be sad too. It can help to make a note of when you find yourself feeling a bit better and what you were doing – maybe going for a walk, talking to a family member, reading a book, baking a cake, or listening to music. Then you can try to do that thing more often, and it will help to get you through each day. Focus on your life. It still exists. When we lose someone we need to make sure another life is not taken – meaning that yours still goes on in its own special and meaningful way, with happy times as well as sad times. And if these words make you want to scream and shout with rage because you don't want to do any of this or think anything positive yet, then don't! Find somewhere to scream and shout instead. The key thing is to allow yourself to feel whatever you feel. If you do that, one day the memories that are too painful at the moment will become the most comforting things – things that will make you grateful for the time you had with your mum. And the comfort you want from her will suddenly arrive, as if from her, but in a new and more extraordinary way – you'll be giving it to yourself.

I'm so sorry that you feel let down by your friends. I'm going to tell you something an author and agony aunt I admire once told a grieving mother, which really stuck with me. Cheryl Strayed told the mother not to worry about how other people perceived her grief because she was living on 'planet My Baby Died'. Your friends live on planet Earth. You live on planet My Mum Died. Don't be afraid to live on planet My Mum Died. Your friends are saying silly things about their parents and complaining about them, because we all do that – we complain about those we love even though we don't ever want to lose them. They are forgetting what you have been through and focusing on their own problems – like getting grounded, or not being allowed dessert until they've finished all their vegetables – and understandably this is very frustrating to you. You would do anything to have those problems instead of the one you do have. While I'm sure your friends will try to be there for you and sympathise with you, they won't ever be able to fully understand your situation, and you can't expect them to either. They will be worrying about their own lives, as we all do. And as time passes, people will probably forget about your grief and assume you are OK. It's tough to realise and accept this, but if you remove your need for your friends to 'get it', you might find you can have fun with them when you want to, the way you always have – doing the things you enjoy doing with them, talking to them, hanging out. But that doesn't mean you don't need people to talk to who do 'get it'.

I suggest you try to see a counsellor or use one of the relevant helplines at the back of this book. Perhaps you have already received some help for your grief, but you are allowed to continue with this. No one expects you to just 'get over it' after a short amount of time. There is help available for young people like yourself who have lost parents or other loved ones. Your life has changed. There will always be a part of you grieving for your mother. You may find you need ongoing help for this. But your life isn't over, and you can still have happiness and fulfilment in your future. She may not be with you physically, but your mum will always be a part of who you are.

Love,
Katie xxx

NOTES

_____

_____

_____

_____

_____

_____

_____

_____

_____

_____

_____

_____

_____

_____

_____

_____

> "CHANGE CAN BE VERY UNSETTLING, HOWEVER INEVITABLE IT IS IN OUR LIVES, BUT YOU ARE STILL YOU."

Dear Katie,

I want to tell you about problems that people like me feel who have moved from another country. Firstly there are language problems. I feel like a small child who doesn't know how to speak or reply to questions. I am afraid to get it wrong so I just keep quiet. Another problem is that I feel completely different because my life has changed – a new country, a new society that I must adapt to when I haven't got my friends to share personal things with. I am having problems with my dad – he isn't in the country right now. We came to England a year ago and I haven't seen him since. I am worried because I have a really hard time talking and communicating with him. When I call him I really don't know what to say. Also, some people

from other countries get picked on – some of
the boys make fun of the girls who wear headscarves.
What should I do to help the girls who wear a scarf?

From Me

Hey You,

Not being able to speak the language of the country
you're in must be very frustrating – and you've described
it perfectly by saying that it makes you feel as though
you're a young child only just learning to talk. I think I
would feel the same. It's important that you share how
you feel with family and teachers, and ask them if they
can explain this to your friends and classmates so that
they can help you. On holiday once I met a girl from
Germany – she only spoke German and I only spoke
English. We somehow managed to have a friendship
on the holiday despite her only knowing three English
words and me knowing no German words at all. The only
shared language we had was 'play' 'eat' and 'drink'.
So we did play, eat and drink. We made sandcastles on
the beach and ate ice creams and managed to get on
quite well, despite it being frustrating at times because
conversation is such a great part of life. I've no doubt

that your English will improve, particularly since many people around you are speaking it, and soon you will be able to make friends and have fun with them, but I'm telling you this story because I wonder in the meantime if you can use a means of translation to help. For example, you could use translation sites on the internet or a language dictionary to communicate with people and request their patience. Talk to your teachers and ask them to help you to ensure you can not only learn at school but also make friends and have fun with them. I have met children in schools who don't speak English and their English-speaking friends have looked out for them and been patient with them. It makes me very happy to see that. There are helplines at the back of this book for people in your position – perhaps you can join a group and talk to others who speak your language and are in the same situation. You're not the only one and it is always a relief and so comforting to have a moan with people who are experiencing the same frustrations as us!

It's upsetting to hear that some people pick on people from other countries at your school. You are a caring person to ask what you can do to help the girls who are bullied for wearing headscarves. Stand up for them if you feel safe to do so, and if you don't feel comfortable with that then tell a teacher when you see this happening instead. Looking out for others will set a great example and encourage others to do the same, and will hopefully make your school more inclusive.

It is totally understandable that you have been feeling unstable due to the changes in your life. It must be extremely difficult to deal with everything in your life changing at once. We all go through changes but they don't always come at once – people move house, lose family members, move away from friends, go from primary school to high school – but what most of what you know has changed, including your culture. Ideas, customs and behaviours might be very different here to how they were in your country, which can make adapting to a new environment and meeting new people even harder. Concentrate on the things that you have control over, and which are never going to change – unless you want them to – yourself and your actions. Remind yourself that home can be anywhere, and that your identity remains the same, no matter what else changes and where you are. Change can be very unsettling, however inevitable it is in our lives, but you are still YOU. Do my exercise on page 79 and write down all the things that make you who you are. You can still be the person you want to be, no matter where you are. Remember all the things that make you brilliant and focus on other constants in your life – the family members you do have with you, an object you've brought from home. Can you start up any hobbies you had in your home country, play music you used to listen to, or read a book from home?

I'm so sorry to hear that you're struggling to communicate with your dad. You must be missing him hugely. But you do call him, and that's the most important thing, even if you don't know what to say. I can imagine it must be tough to find things to talk to him about and keep your relationship the same as it was. This can be especially tricky when you're speaking to someone on the phone and not face to face.

To help with this, I suggest you keep a diary of everything you do each day. Your new experiences – what you've eaten, what you've done in school, who you've spoken to and how you've felt. Then when you call your dad you can refer to this diary and keep him up to date with what's been going on with you. Tell him things that have happened, even if you think they don't seem particularly exciting – they will keep the conversation going and might lead you on to other things. I'm sure your dad is missing you just as much, and wants to know exactly what you're up to and paint a picture of it in his head. Ask him questions too – enquire about his day and what he's been doing. You can ask him for advice about whatever you're going through, such as telling him what you've told me – about your struggles with language at school and how all the changes in your life are making you feel unsettled. Ask him what he would do if he were you. Talking to your dad about these things might just solve all the problems you've written to me about. After all, your dad does speak your language, so you can communicate with him and tell him the things you might not be able to tell people at your new school. The key to ensuring you stay close to someone is to keep communicating – whatever it is you talk about.

Take your life here one day at a time, and don't expect or force yourself to feel completely integrated and settled in straight away. It's going to be a gradual process. Keep that diary, focus on one hour to the next and one obstacle at a time. Things will get easier.

Love,
Katie xxx

Dear Katie,

I have a brother who has ADHD. This makes him hard to deal with and he can become aggressive. We always argue and have fights, and if he hits me first I hit him back. When I do this I get the blame and my brother starts lying about what happened and I get in more trouble. What would you do?

How should I solve this problem? How should I act towards my brother?

From Me

Hey You,

I sympathise with you because it must be tricky to have a sibling with a health condition which affects their behaviour and consequently has an impact on you.

Since you've written to me about this you clearly care about your brother but you are frustrated, because although he has a particular set of needs, you have needs too. Do not feel ashamed for finding this situation difficult – anyone would. Allow yourself to feel how you feel.

Your parents probably find looking after your brother hard at times, but they will still love and care about both of you. Speak to them, without your brother around, and tell them how you feel. Rather than complaining, explain that you understand your brother needs specific care but that certain aspects of your relationship are getting you down. Your parents might be able to suggest ways to make life easier.

It's important to remember that your brother might not always be able to control his actions, so although it must be frustrating when he hits you and this makes you want to hit him back, try not to. Like you said, you are the one who then gets in trouble, and while this seems unfair, it is probably because your parents know that you have more control over those decisions than your brother. ADHD sufferers can be susceptible to periods of aggression, so try to take this into account. Can you speak to someone about ways of dealing with the situation when your brother gets aggressive, such as calmly walking away?

Spend time with your family and enjoy their company, help out your mum and dad, and speak to them about the best way to deal with your brother. Your family is a team, and the best way to cope with situations like this is to remain a team and keep talking and doing things together. That doesn't mean you always have to be with them – spending time with friends, doing hobbies or going to after-school clubs will give you a break from your home environment, and some space from it will give you patience and help you deal with difficulties when you are at home.

Radha has provided advice about ADHD – I'm sure you already know lots about it, so this is as much for other readers as it is for you. Saying that, it might help you to understand your brother better and think about how best you can support him while also looking after yourself – your happiness matters too.

Love,
Katie xxx

DR RADHA SAYS

ADHD is the most commonly diagnosed behavioural disorder of children. It's associated with a number of different symptoms which fall under three main categories:

- Difficulty controlling what you say or do (impulsivity)
- Difficulty in keeping attention or concentration (inattention)
- Unable to sit still (hyperactivity)

It is thought 2 – 5% of school age children may have ADHD. Luckily, there are lots of treatments for ADHD. They include special educational support, behavioural therapy, medication, family meetings and counselling.

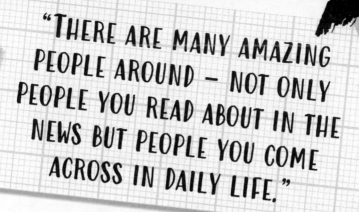

> "THERE ARE MANY AMAZING PEOPLE AROUND — NOT ONLY PEOPLE YOU READ ABOUT IN THE NEWS BUT PEOPLE YOU COME ACROSS IN DAILY LIFE."

Dear Katie,

I am scared with all the terrorism going on. I don't feel safe going to a public school because any old terrorist could walk in and kill us all and I'd never see my family again. I need advice to get over this paranoia.

From Me

Hey You,

I can't tell you not to worry about terrorism, because I'd be a hypocrite. I worry about it. In 2017, a concert full of young people in Manchester was targeted. This was the closest to home terrorism had ever felt to me because I grew up and live in Manchester. For the first few weeks – maybe even months – after that attack I felt nervous everywhere I went. I was looking at everyone around me, and feeling vulnerable and claustrophobic whenever I was in a crowded, busy place.

I worry about terrorism in the same way that I worry about all the awful things which may or may not happen to me or my loved ones. While initially after such an incident your sense of awareness and fear are heightened, once it all settles down I choose to take the view that it's extremely unlikely it will happen to me – and there's little I can do to make sure it doesn't. I don't want to live my life in fear and not enjoy myself because I'm worried about terrorism. This is how terrorism works – fear is the terrorist's weapon of choice. It's not just the people they physically harm in these attacks but the many they harm and control mentally by making people feel scared and powerless. Surveys have shown that after terror attacks people have a more negative world view and elevated stress levels. It isn't fair that we should have to feel this way – we must do all we can to continue living the happy and fulfilling lives that we desire and deserve.

As I said, I can't tell you not to worry. I could give you all the facts and figures which show how very, very unlikely it is you'll ever be caught up in a terror attack, but the most important thing is to not let the worrying stop you from doing what you want to do and from feeling good. You owe that to yourself. Do what I do – try to focus on the good things in the world instead of the bad. There are many amazing people around – not only people you read about in the news but people you come across in daily life. Appreciate whenever you see or hear about someone doing something kind. If you watch or read the news then try to do that less often, or look for positive news stories – some websites and publications focus solely on those but most mainstream news mainly reports on the bad stuff. In fact, why don't you start your own 'good news' magazine? You could turn it into a project to find all the good around you, writing down when you see someone be kind or helpful or when you hear about something wonderful happening to someone. This will change your perspective and make you feel more positive and optimistic about the world. Often we do the opposite of this and focus on the doom and gloom.

If your parents watch the news and you find the stories are scaring or worrying you then leave the room when it's on. Because we have regular access to everything going on in the world, watching the news can make us think that ONLY bad stuff ever happens. I have reduced how much news I watch in order to be as happy and stress-free as possible. We humans seem to have a fascination with the negative things in the world – a morbid curiosity. We allow them to dominate our conversations and can exaggerate things to make them sound scarier or more likely or more terrible.

It's understandable to be scared and worried about events that have happened in the world, and you shouldn't bottle your feelings up. You can speak to your friends, but sometimes they can egg us on and wind us up and make us feel even more anxious, so I suggest talking to a parent or teacher or school counsellor about how you're feeling. An adult with a good understanding of what's going on in the world will listen to you, tell you the facts and help you to reduce your worries.

Kids' show host Fred Rogers once said something which I'd like you to remember: "When I was a boy and I would see scary things in the news, my mother would say to me, 'Look for the helpers. You can always find people who are helping.'"

Love,
Katie xxx

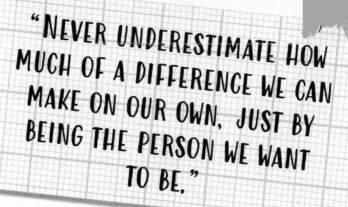

> "NEVER UNDERESTIMATE HOW MUCH OF A DIFFERENCE WE CAN MAKE ON OUR OWN, JUST BY BEING THE PERSON WE WANT TO BE."

Dear Katie,

Some children go to school every day yet don't appreciate the opportunities they have, since many people are living in poverty and don't have the chance to be educated. How can I show others that there is a point to school? My siblings think it's silly, however I disagree and I think school is great. Do you have any ideas about how I can show school to them in a different perspective so that they begin to enjoy it?

From Me

Dear Katie,

I feel like there's not enough care and support for the people who are less fortunate, and I wish I could do something about it. I wish that people would stop treating others differently just because they are not as rich or because they don't have expensive things. I wish everyone could treat people with love and respect and have peace.

From Me

Dear Katie,

I would like to save the remaining half of the Great Barrier Reef in Australia but I can't think of anything I can do that will help fix it. When I'm older I want to be a marine biologist and it is my dream to explore the Great Barrier Reef, and I'm worried there won't be much to explore.

From Me

Dear Katie,

Whenever I go to the town centre I see homeless people littered across the busy streets and they hardly get any money. Because I'm a kid I can't do much to help the poor souls but I give them food on a regular basis and some change. My question is: do you feel the same?

From Me

Hello my superheroes,

I was bowled over by your letters, and the many more I received like these from other young people who in some way want to help make the world a better place.

Sometimes we wish we had so much power to do something extreme – to end poverty, to buy every homeless person a house, to save all the endangered wildlife – but these things are not within our reach. Sometimes this can make us feel helpless, but we should never underestimate how much of a difference we can make on our own, just by being the person we want to be. By being the person we want everyone to be.

You can be the person who buys a homeless person a sandwich and smiles at them, who doesn't waste electricity, who is enthusiastic about going to school and learning new things every day, who is kind to everyone they meet – rich or poor, black or white, old or young, happy or sad. Be the person who opens doors for others, who asks someone you see fall over if they're OK, who helps an elderly person with their bags, who talks to the person sitting alone at lunchtime, who sticks up for the bully victim and is also kind to the bully . . .

You might not be able to cure world hunger all on your own, but you can do more than you think you can. Just a smile can do so much. A smile, a conversation, a helpful hand will make a difference to someone's life.

Spread the messages you have told me about, and you will influence others and make the world a much better place, by existing and by being you. I promise. Your worth and influence is more than you think it is.

Don't forget that being selfish is also OK. Not in the sense of intentionally harming others through selfishness, but by making sure you are happy and healthy first and foremost. We can't help others if we're struggling ourselves.

I've no doubt that each and every one of you is already changing the world for the better.

Love,
Katie xxx

NOTES

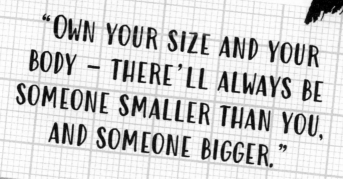

> "OWN YOUR SIZE AND YOUR BODY — THERE'LL ALWAYS BE SOMEONE SMALLER THAN YOU, AND SOMEONE BIGGER."

Dear Katie,

My problem is my weight because my family says I'm underweight and sometimes my sister takes the mick out of me and calls me 'twiggy'. This really upsets me. Has anyone ever taken the mick out of your weight?

From Me

Dear Katie,

Why am I fat? People at school make fun of me because of it. I just can't stop eating. Is it my hormones?

From Me

Hey Both of You,

I wanted to answer your letters together because you're both experiencing people making remarks about your weight and it's making you feel unhappy. I thought it might be interesting for both of you to see that the problem – of other people making remarks – exists regardless of your size or shape or weight, or anything else to do with your appearance. However we look, we may encounter people saying unkind things about us and our appearance, whether or not they realise their words are hurtful.

To the first letter: the remarks are coming from your family and sometimes this can be seen as friendly 'banter' between siblings or from a parent to a child. But if it's upsetting you then you should treat it as you would if people at school were picking on you – as in the case of letter two. Speak to your family about the remarks because, although they might not realise it, this sort of 'friendly' name-calling gets into our psyche. It can change the way we feel about ourselves and affect our confidence. I don't believe that anyone should tell somebody else how or who they are, as it can affect the way that person feels about themselves. Choose the family member you think will be most understanding, and have a serious chat with them. Tell them how it makes you feel and show them this letter. Tell them that Katie said they need to stop.

To the second letter: the people making fun of you aren't people you need to have in your life. Try and separate yourself from them as best you can and only spend time with people who make you feel good – everything in life is a choice and who we choose to spend time with has a huge effect on our mood. If you want to make some new friends, there are lots of tips in this book about how to do so. Perhaps join a club to make new, like-minded friends and build your confidence. Talk to your teacher, if people continue to make fun of you, because this should be stopped.

In answer to the question: YES, people have picked on me because of my weight before. I've only really experienced this since becoming a TV presenter. I've had people tweet me to tell me that I've either lost or put on weight, and I've had people ask me if I'm pregnant because my tummy looks bigger! I'd like to tell you that it doesn't upset me, but it does. Someone once commented on one of my Instagram photos to tell me I'm fat and ugly. Thanks for that!

The best way to deal with this kind of situation is to realise that other people's opinions of you don't matter. For that reason, I don't suggest either of you to try to change your appearance – put on or lose weight. If these comments offend you and you're otherwise happy and healthy then I'd advise you to try some self-confidence exercises, such as smiling at yourself in the mirror and listing things you like about yourself. Own your size and your body – there'll always be someone smaller than you, and someone bigger – and there'll be someone somewhere who wishes they looked like you. When I think of the people I find most attractive, it's usually their confidence that is so striking. I know women larger in size who are super-confident and all you see when you look at them is an attractive woman who is loving life. On the other hand, I know people who put hours and hours of work into how they look, talk about their 'body goals' on social media, but are so uncomfortable and unconfident in themselves that it shows in the way they stand, speak, behave. If you're happy with how you eat, exercise, live, look, then embrace that and forget everyone else.

However, if the comments hurt you because they remind you that you ARE unhappy with your body and you think you might be eating unhealthily and therefore putting on or losing weight, then make an appointment with your GP. To the second letter: you mention that you can't stop eating. This is nothing to be ashamed of, nor is undereating. Many of us have a difficult relationship with food and it can be really tricky to manage. I struggle with comfort eating, and I share your frustrations. Radha's information about emotional eating and eating disorders should help – it's advice that most of us can benefit from. Our bodies and minds and relationships with food are extremely complex, and struggling with this is only human.

Love,
Katie xxx

DR RADHA SAYS

Emotional overeating is when we eat large amounts of food because we are experiencing intense negative feelings or thoughts. We are not physically hungry but are eating as a response to our feelings. Sometimes these feelings may be related to a negative body image or pressure to lose weight. These feelings can often come on suddenly, with intense cravings for sugary or fatty food that we feel we need to eat right this moment. The cravings may not stop even when we are full, and we can feel ashamed or guilty afterwards. Emotional overeating is often something people do as a way to cope with their distressing or intense negative feelings.

There is help out there for people who may be emotionally overeating, and the best thing to do is to recognise if this is a problem for you and to seek help from your GP. Often once the pattern of thinking and feeling is recognised, then it can be broken, with expert help and support.

"FORGIVE YOURSELF AND ACCEPT."

Dear Katie,

If you hurt somebody really badly and you couldn't fix it, what would you do?

From Me

Hey You,

I have hurt somebody badly in the past and I haven't been able to fix it. Mostly in relationships in my adult life. I've started relationships with people who other people wanted to date and it has hurt those people. I've ended relationships and it hurt those people. I've also had these things done to me and been hurt lots too.

I'm not sure how you have hurt this person, but we will all hurt someone at some point in our lives, whether we intend to or not.

We mustn't set out to hurt other people, but our decisions sometimes cause hurt and this is, sadly, a part of life. Did you hurt this person in order to avoid hurting yourself? If so, try not to beat yourself up about it, because you had no other choice.

If you could have avoided hurting this person but did so anyway, for whatever reason, then the first thing to do is accept that this has happened. You can't turn back time, so accept it and say out loud: "I hurt this person." The next thing to do is make sure you are no longer doing whatever it was that hurt them, and have done all you can to stop them hurting. Then you can say out loud: "I hurt this person, but I did everything I possibly could to ensure they suffered minimum pain." This will involve apologising and speaking to them about what happened. Explain your actions and do whatever you can to make them feel better. You might decide to write them a letter – either to send to them or for yourself, to work through your feelings. Or you can write a diary entry about what happened, what you learned from it and what you would do differently in the future. These experiences teach us about ourselves and about life, and will make you a better person. Then let it go. You've done all you can, and the outcome is out of your control.

The final step is to forgive yourself and accept that either you hurt someone because you had no choice or that you did something wrong and hurt someone as a consequence. Whichever one it is, focus now on moving on, because if you are hurting too, that's two lives affected instead of one – feeling continuously guilty will stop you from feeling happy and fulfilled. The person you have hurt will themselves work on feeling better and forgetting about what happened, and you must do the same. You can learn from this experience and go about your life as a better person because of what happened.

You're not a bad person.

Love,
Katie xxx

JUST IN CASE NO ONE HAS
TOLD YOU TODAY,
YOU ARE GOOD ENOUGH

HELPLINES

There is always help available. If the symptoms below sound like you or someone you know, don't suffer in silence:

Lacking energy or feeling tired | Feeling tearful, restless or agitated | Not wanting to talk to or be with people | Not wanting to do things you usually enjoy | Taking or thinking about taking drugs or a lot of alcohol | Finding it hard to cope with everyday things | Thoughts or urges to self-harm or feeling suicidal | Thinking about running away | At risk of being abused or hurt

If you need help or just need to talk, try contacting one of these numbers or visiting one of these websites.

Anxiety UK
Support for people with anxiety conditions
Call: 08444 775 774 (9.30am-5.30pm, Monday – Friday)
Website: www.anxietyuk.org.uk

Beat
Support for people suffering from eating disorders
Call: 0808 801 0711 (for under-18s) (3:30pm-10:00pm everday)
Website: www.b-eat.co.uk

Bipolar UK
Help for people living with manic depression or bipolar disorder
Call: 0333 323 3880 (9:00am-5:00pm, Monday – Friday)
Website: www.bipolaruk.org.uk

Coram Voice
Support for children in care or in need of help from Children's Services
Call: 0808 800 5792 (9.30am–6pm, Monday – Friday; 10am–4pm, Saturday)
WhatsApp: +44 (0)7758 670369
Email: help@coramvoice.org.uk
Website: www.coramvoice.org.uk

Childline
Private and confidential service for people up to the age of 19 on any issue
Call: 0800 1111 (24 hours a day)
Online chat: www.childline.org.uk/Talk/Chat/Pages/OnlineChat.aspx
Website: www.childline.org.uk

Child Bereavement
Bereavement support
Call: 0800 02 888 40 (9:00am–5:00pm, Monday – Friday)
Email: support@childbereavementuk.org
Website: www.childbereavementuk.org

Hope Again

Bereavement support for young people
Call: 0808 808 1677 (9:30am – 5:00pm, Monday – Friday)
Email: hopeagain@cruse.org.uk
Website: www.hopeagain.org.uk

Mind

Support for mental health
Call: 0300 123 3393 (9:00am – 6:00pm, Monday – Friday
(except for bank holidays))
Text: 86463
Website: www.mind.org.uk

No Panic

Support for sufferers of panic attacks and OCD
Call: 0330 606 1174 (3:00pm – 6:00pm, Monday – Friday;
6:00pm – 8:00pm, Thursday and Saturday)
Website: www.nopanic.org.uk

OCD Action

Support for people with OCD
Call: 0845 390 6232 (9.30am – 5:00pm, Monday – Friday)
Website: www.ocdaction.org.uk

Papyrus
Suicide prevention for young people
Call: 0800 068 4141 (10:00am – 10:00pm, Monday – Friday;
2:00pm –10:00pm Weekends; 2:00pm – 5:00pm, Bank
Holidays)
Text: 07786 209697
Email: pat@papyrus–uk.org
Website: www.papyrus-uk.org

Refuge
Support for those experiencing domestic violence
Call: 0808 2000 247 (24 hours a day)
Website: www.refuge.org.uk

Samaritans
Offering emotional support on any issue
Call: 116 123 (24 hours a day)
Website: www.samaritans.org

Safeline
Support for those that have experienced sexual violence
Call: 0800 800 5007 (10:00am – 4:00pm, Monday,
Wednesday, Friday; 8:00am – 8:00 pm, Tuesday, Thursday;
10:00am – 12:00pm Saturday)
Text: 0786 002 7573
Website: www.safeline.org.uk

Sane Line

Offering specialist mental health emotional support
Call: 0300 304 7000 (4:30pm – 10:30pm every day)
Website: www.sane.org.uk

Stonewall

Information and support for LGBT communities and their allies
Call: 08000 50 20 20 (9:30am – 5:30pm, Monday – Friday)
Email: info@stonewall.org.uk
Website: www.stonewall.org.uk

Victim Support

Support for people affected by crime and traumatic events
Call: 0808 168 9111 (24 hours a day)
Website: www.victimsupport.org

PLACE2BE

Katie is an active mental health campaigner and champions the importance of supporting children's emotional wellbeing at school. She is an ambassador for the children's mental health charity Place2Be.

Place2Be is the UK's leading children's mental health charity providing in-school support and expert training to improve the emotional wellbeing of pupils, families, teachers and school staff.

This support helps young people to cope with wide-ranging and often complex issues including bullying, bereavement, domestic violence, family breakdown, neglect and trauma.

Place2Be's school-based teams build strong links with students, staff and parents to help develop a 'mentally healthy' ethos within the school environment.

The charity also trains school leaders, teachers and mental health professionals to build their understanding of children's mental health and wellbeing.

To find out more visit www.place2be.org.uk

Registered charity numbers 1040756 and SC038649

NOTES

p. 94. 'It wasn't very easy – growing up. 'Venus was like a model. I was thicker.' Serena Williams to the *Huffington Post*, 2015. http://www. huffingtonpost.co.uk/entry/serena-williams-body-image_n_7599214

p. 94 '[Casting agents] would say, "You're just not what we're looking for Kate."' Kate Winslet at We Day U.K. charity event in London, 2017. https:// www.vanityfair.com/style/2017/03/kate-winslet-speech-bullying

p. 94 'I realised it's because I can't even reconcile myself with my own image on the front of these magazines' Emma Watson to *Esquire*, 2016. http:// www.esquire.co.uk/culture/news/a9624/esquire-meets-emma-watson/

p. 94 'My overriding memory of that time is the slowly evaporating sense of self-esteem' J. K. Rowling for *Gingerbread*, http://gingerbreadweb. wpengine.com/community/stories/i-prouder-years-single-mother-part-life/

p. 287 'You live on Planet My Baby Died.' Cheryl Strayed (as Sugar) for *The Rumpus*. http://therumpus.net/2010/07/dear-sugar-the-rumpus-advice-column-44-how-you-get-unstuck/

p. 304 'He was always comforted by something his mother would tell him during times of disaster: "Look for the helpers. You can always find people who are helping."' Fred Rogers quoted in *The New York Times*. https://www.nytimes.com/2017/08/30/learning/look-for-the-helpers.html

NOTES